How To Present To Absolutely Anyone

How To Present To Absolutely Anyone

Confident Public Speaking and Presenting in Every Situation

Mark Rhodes

CAPSTONE
A Wiley Brand

Registered office
John Wiley & Sons Ltd, The Atrium, Southern Gate, Chichester, West Sussex, PO19 8SQ, United Kingdom

For details of our global editorial offices, for customer services and for information about how to apply for permission to reuse the copyright material in this book please see our website at www.wiley.com.

Library of Congress Cataloging-in-Publication Data

Names: Rhodes, Mark, 1966- author.
Title: How to present to absolutely anyone : confident public speaking and presenting in every situation / Mark Rhodes.
Description: West Sussex : Wiley-Capstone, 2019. | Includes index. |
    Identifiers: LCCN 2018035675 (print) | LCCN 2018045263 (ebook) |
    ISBN 9780857087768 (Adobe PDF) | ISBN 9780857087744 (ePub) |
    ISBN 9780857087737 (pbk.) | ISBN 9780857087768 (ePDF)
Subjects: LCSH: Public speaking. | Business presentations.
Classification: LCC PN4129.15 (ebook) | LCC PN4129.15 .R485 2019 (print) |
    DDC 808.5/1—dc23
LC record available at https://lccn.loc.gov/2018035675

Cover Design: Wiley

Set in 11.5/15pt Adobe Caslon Pro-Regular by SPi Global, Chennai, India

Printed in Great Britain by TJ International Ltd, Padstow, Cornwall, UK

10 9 8 7 6 5 4 3 2 1

With special thanks to Mike Ward who not only took a chance and gave me my first official speaking engagement, but also helped massively with my confidence when he said some simple yet powerful words as I came off stage:

"Mark, you are a really good speaker"

Contents

CONTENTS

Foreword

I've had the pleasure of knowing and working with Mark for a number of years, I'm delighted to contribute to the Foreword on *How To Present To Absolutely Anyone*.

On many occasions in the past, I have invited Mark to speak at events; more predominantly whilst he was one of the 'Millionaire Mentors' on the EBA with James Caan.

Unfailingly articulate and engaging as a speaker, Mark has always managed to entertain and inform his audience; keeping the room fully focussed on his message at any time.

On a personal level, I was once amazed when he'd told me of his past fear of public speaking. His delivery has always been so relaxed and confident; drawing the audience in, I'd never have believed he had endured years of fear in this area. This is why this book is just so good; it's a pocket-sized testament to Mark's journey - packed with information, advice and Mark's experiences which will assist the reader in their own journey to perfect presentations. Its quite possibly the only presenting book you will ever need.

Bev James
Best Selling Author of Do it! Or Ditch it and
CEO of The Coaching Academy.

1
How to Deliver Presentations Without Fear, That You and Your Audience Will Love and You'll Enjoy Doing

I know this chapter title probably sounds like quite a big claim right now, but this book is about a process and system that I've developed over the last eight to ten years, where I've managed to take myself from somebody who'd never do a talk or presentation anywhere, to someone who is now in demand around the world as a speaker – and who always gets great reviews and feedback from the audience and the event organisers. But, more importantly, I never get nervous these days and actually look forward to doing presentations and talks!

Now, I know many of you reading this won't necessarily be aiming for a career in public speaking – or being a paid speaker as such – you just want to add the skills of speaking and presenting to what you already do.

There can be nothing better than being able to stand up in front of a room of people and deliver a message. A message that inspires or motivates people, or maybe a message that gets people interested in what you or your organisation does. A message you hope will get the audience to take some action afterwards and perhaps even engage with you in a transaction or on some other level.

Being able to do this can also make you the envy of your peers and associates, because so many people in the world would never do what you are about to be able to do.

The ability to confidently deliver a message to a group of people is empowering. After all, great speeches in history have moved millions of people and created a future very different to how it would have been without those speeches.

As I write this, I am reminded of two speaking engagements that I did recently on the exact same topic. One was on a Monday and the other was the very next day on the Tuesday.

At the event on the Tuesday, when I was introduced the audience applauded and looked excited for me to be there, despite the fact that they had not met me before and they didn't even know an external speaker was going to present to them that day at their event.

It was a very different experience to the day before, the Monday, when after being introduced I walked to the front of the room in silence, no applause, just deadly silence!

What is even more interesting about this is experience is that the Monday group had heard me speak to them five months before, they had loved my presentation so much that they had to get me back again to share even more with them . . . and yet there was no applause as I went up to the front of the room.

Why was this?

After all, you could understand it if it had happened the other way around. A crowd that had heard me before and loved me had given me huge applause and the Tuesday group who'd never met me had just stayed quiet.

Interesting. Well, in fact the difference was, quite simply, how I was introduced. Both introductions were very short but the words used and the tonality used were very different. The introductions were very short presentations themselves with very different outcomes, despite being about the same topic – me.

At the Monday event, when it came to my slot the person introducing me simply said in a monotone voice: 'Mark spoke back in July and has come back today to share more with us, so I will now hand over to Mark'.

At the Tuesday event, the person introducing me said in an excited voice: 'Really pleased Mark is here today to share ideas on Transformational Leadership, please give a warm welcome to Mark'.

So, a different tonality and a few different words 'hand over to Mark' vs 'a warm welcome to Mark' – these four or five words and how they were said made the difference between 80 people clapping and looking excited and 80 people sitting in a deadly silence.

A lot of presentations and talks that people deliver have their whole 30 or 60 minutes delivered like that Monday introduction. A much smaller percentage of presentations are delivered with the words and tonality that move people in unimaginable ways.

So this is why public speaking – and doing it correctly – is so powerful and so important. Not to mention rewarding!

Now, when I say doing it correctly, I don't mean there are 101 tips coming up in this book on what to do and what not to do when you are at the front of a room delivering a message.

What you have here is a process and way of developing yourself and your content so that delivering content or a message is easy and the audience are always engaged with both you and your content.

Everywhere I go and deliver my own presentations, I hear from so many people who want to develop this skill further and get better at doing this. Both from the standpoint of reducing their fear, if they've got fear, and of getting better results from the presentations that they do.

In my experience, people want to deliver a presentation that they are going to look forward to delivering and that they know the audience is going to like, enjoy and get value from.

I have heard it said that when people are surveyed about their biggest fears, the fear of public speaking ranks higher than the fear of death. And I also heard somebody once say that this means that at a funeral, most people would rather be in the box going in the ground than standing at the top reading the eulogy!

Now, I'm sure it's not that bad. I'm sure none of us would actually wish that in reality – although it might feel like that when the dreaded fear and feelings of impending doom strike when it is not something you are comfortable doing.

So I have written this book for all those people who tell me they want to be able to present with confidence, like I do, and know the steps I take to be able to deliver great presentations.

When I ask what stage they're at with public speaking, I realise most of the time that they are far more advanced than I was when I started out doing presentations. I'm not sure it is possible for anyone to be more scared than I once was.

Because they are far more advanced than I was, I know that I can easily help them to fast track what they're doing and to get far better than they currently are and far better results than they're currently getting. And that's the reason I've decided to put down everything I know, have done and continue to do, in this book.

This book is also for you even if you've never done a presentation before.

There are also free videos to support this book, which you can access at https://www.markrhodes.com/public-speaking-videos

How Did I Start Out With Presentations and Overcome My Own Fears?

I was desperate. I'd spent years fearing presentations and done some pretty extreme things to avoid them, even to the point where I once faked a car accident to make an excuse for not attending a meeting where I was due to give one. More on that a little later.

I knew that something had to change, that I had to master this. That I'd spent too many years running away from presentations, making excuses, and it was something that I needed to do.

I realised that I'd had success in other parts of my life – I had even started, grown and sold a business successfully – and yet I was still running away from doing presentations with dread and fear.

And, you know, I then figured it out.

I figured out what I needed to do in order to reduce the fear and in order to develop great content. So much so that today, I just love it. I absolutely love public speaking. I don't even get nervous anymore.

This has led to me speaking on many big stages around the world. I've spoken in Hong Kong, Dubai, the USA, countries across Europe. So many places.

I've spoken for major well-known brands and received amazing feedback and testimonials. Again, this is just to show you how far I've come from the person who was too scared to do a talk and didn't know the first step in putting a talk together.

I've had two books published by a major publisher and out in the shops. I have also been featured in lots of press and media – and all of this has come about because of my speaking. My speaking has led to everything else.

I know that you might not be looking to become a speaker or write books, but I'm sharing this with you to show you the extent of the changes I've made from somebody who was totally fearful of doing presentations to someone who's in demand as a speaker.

I'm sharing this with you as a way to get you to believe that you too can get better at public speaking and presentations.

You can reduce that fear.

You can develop that content that you and your audience will love.

Do not think for one minute that you're just not the sort of person to do this, because no matter where you are with your own public speaking skills or confidence levels, I'm sure, as I said earlier, you are further on than I was when I started out.

So how did I do it? How bad was I? and how did I make that transformation?

Let's start with how bad I was.

On leaving college I got my first job in a firm of accountants. I'd been there for about six months when the manager said to me,

> 'Mark, the supervisor is off today, you need to go to Head Office and represent our office. And at the meeting, you're going to be in a room of about 12 people, and you're going to have to stand up for about a minute and read out from this sheet of paper what we've been doing in our office.'

And I thought,

> 'That's it, I'm not doing that. Absolutely no way. I'm not standing up and doing a talk, you can forget that.'

But then I realised pretty quickly that when your boss tells you you've got to do something, you've probably got to do it. And not only that, I was only 18. It was my first job after leaving college, so I thought, 'I better do this'.

So I set off to Head Office in my car on this dreadful day. The closer I got to the venue, the hotter I got; the fear was getting worse and worse the closer I got to the venue.

I got about 100 yards from that building, and I thought: 'I can't do this. There's absolutely no way. I can't do this. I'm not going'. Then I had a brilliant idea. I thought, 'I know what I'll do, I'll tell them I've had an accident in the car and I'll have to miss the meeting because I've got to wait for the police!'

So that's what I did. We didn't have mobile phones or cellphones in those days, so I went to the nearest phone box, I phoned up the office and said: 'I'm really sorry, somebody has hit my car. I've got to wait for the police. I'm not going to be able to make the meeting'.

They said, 'Don't worry Mark, the important thing is are you safe? Are you okay?' (I was feeling a bit guilty at this point for lying to my employer and the fact that they were worrying about my safety when there was absolutely nothing wrong with me – other than the complete fear of doing that one-minute talk of course!)

They told me to sort things out and then go home and they'd see me tomorrow at the office and I wasn't to worry about missing the meeting.

Result!

When I got back home, I went through two phases.

The first was that I was really happy, really excited, really proud of myself because I had yet again got out of doing a talk or speaking in public.

Then the next phase I went through was, 'Oh no, when I go in to work tomorrow they will see that there's nothing wrong with my car'.

I then had to go out with a hammer and break the back lights on my own car, just to create evidence of this so-called accident that never happened!

That's how scared I was and the extent I would go to so I could avoid doing a one-minute presentation, in public, to a room of 12 people!

That's how bad I was at speaking in public. But these days, I will stand on stage for an hour plus with 1000 people or more in the audience, no slides, and I'll love every single minute of it. In fact, when I look down at my stopwatch and see I've only got five minutes left of my time on stage, I'm disappointed it's going to be over so soon.

So, what changed?

What changed to make me go from one extreme to the other?

2
My Change: From Extreme Public Speaking Fear to Total Confidence

After I achieved my success in business, I was completely astounded that I'd managed it; building a company and eventually selling it to a large Silicon Valley organisation in the USA.

I then got curious about success and how I'd become successful.

I read a number of books, I went on some courses. And I realised most of the things I was reading or hearing I had already been doing naturally, but in my own way, which had also led to my success so far.

What I also realised is that there were some things in my life that I was doing really, really well. Like sales; I was always good at selling and winning new business. And yet there were other things in my life I was doing badly, or not at all; like public speaking.

I eventually realised that the difference between these two things, as soft and simple as it might sound, was how I was thinking about them. I was thinking about them very differently.

You see, when I was going to a sales meeting to see a potential client or customer, I'd be thinking about everything going right. My excited and upbeat internal voice and thinking was something along the lines of:

> 'They are going to love what we do. I can't wait to get there. I can't wait to tell them about our product, about our team. They're going to love us, they're going to want to work with us, they're going to see that we can transform their business and help them go to another level.'

That was my thought process – and thinking like that I felt pretty good when I arrived at those meetings. And I therefore got excellent results most of the time, and my sales conversion or winning rate was very high.

Now, when it came to giving a talk, and somebody said, 'Mark, will you do a talk? Will you do a presentation?' Instead of thinking about everything going right, I'd think about everything going wrong. I'd think:

> 'Maybe I'll forget my words. Maybe I'll look nervous. Maybe the audience won't like it. Maybe I'll pass out!'

And after I've thought about these fears and talked to myself with my internal voice in a very down and depressed tonality, well, I'm scared – I'm smashing up that car and I'm not going to do a presentation anywhere!

This was the eureka moment for me. When I saw first-hand from my own experiences how the thoughts we have, and how we think about things beforehand, have a major impact on the results we get and how we feel during the process – no matter what we are doing.

I then started to change how I was thinking about giving presentations, and I would think more about things going right than things going wrong, and that's when the fear started to diminish for me. I will explain exactly how I made this change as we go through this book.

The fear diminished to a stage that I managed to put myself on a course . . . it wasn't a public speaking course, but it was a course where I'd have to stand up and do a short presentation each day about what we had learnt that day.

Because I had started thinking about things going well with these presentations, imagining myself delivering those talks well, it started to reduce the fear to the point that I'd go on the course and take part in it.

Then the ongoing practice beyond that is what helped me go much further.

In addition to reducing my fears, I also had to come up with ways to develop content and methods of delivery as well as everything else that I'm going to take you through in what I call my 'Zero to Hero in Public Speaking Process'.

Discovering Another Way by Accident

I found out something very interesting some years later when I started helping clients with public speaking and overcoming their own fears, something that made me totally change my original approach.

What I used to do was start by sorting out their mindset and helping them to reduce the fears that were holding them back.

I would say to them at the start of our first coaching session:

'How scared are you on a 0 to 10 scale? Where 0 is I could do a talk right now to a 1000 people. It would be a walk in the park and I'd love every single minute of it. And 10 would be, if I stand up to do a talk, I know I'm going to die!'

Now, because 10 is 'I know I'm going to die', and they know they won't actually die, the most they can choose is 9; although some jokingly still say 10 – but hey, if they are joking now they are not taking it so seriously is often my response, and I tell them they have already made progress! If they had been thinking that they were at a fear level of 10 before our conversation, then I've got an improvement for them already!

Do remember though, when thinking about this fear level for yourself, this scale and judgement of fear level from 0 to 10 is your own personal measurement and only yours. You can't compare it to anyone else – your 7 may be their 9. It is your personal relative scale, so when you check again on another day you will know you have improved if your number has reduced when you think about speaking in public.

But whatever their number was – 7, 8, 9 or whatever on the scale – I would then start to use different techniques to reduce that fear level. Once we got had got their fear level down by various methods to a lower and more manageable number, maybe a 4 or 5, we would then start looking at other areas such as content, delivery style, engaging the audience etc.

Incidentally, this technique of taking our own personal measurement of the level of fear we feel in a given situation is based on the SUD scale concept. SUD stands for Subjective Unit of Distress. The 'D' is also sometimes taken to mean 'Disturbance' or 'Discomfort'. The SUD method was developed by Joseph Wolpe back in 1969.

The great discovery

What I found a couple of years ago, was that I could also do this the other way around! Instead of dealing with their fears first, I could start by looking at their topics and content first.

I realised that a lot of the fears and concerns someone had would massively reduce or go away totally if they knew that they had a really exciting and interesting presentation to deliver, that the audience were going to love it and that they weren't going to make any big mistakes. It would also be even better if they had safety nets in place to make sure that there wouldn't be any major mistakes, or – in the very unlikely situation of something going wrong – that they had a simple strategy or way of dealing with it.

So, as an example, here is something that happened with one of my clients that led me to this realisation: that starting with content and delivery style, as opposed to the fears, also worked brilliantly.

I was asked to go and do some one-to-one coaching to help a young lady who wanted to get better at public speaking. When she first contacted me, her whole focus was about reducing the fear she had. She said to me, 'Mark, I just lack confidence. I've got no confidence to speak in public, and yet I've got to do this big presentation that's coming up'.

She explained that she was going to be doing her presentation to about 60–80 architects, who she said were on average in their 50s with many years of experience, whereas she was a young woman of about 30. I wasn't sure at this stage what the issue was, but it sounded like this in itself was a problem for her.

When we met, I said my usual, 'So tell me on a scale of 0 to 10 how scared you are of doing this presentation, where 0 is it's a walk in the park, I could do it in my sleep and 10 is, I know I'm going to die?'

She replied, 'On a scale of 0 to 10 I'm definitely an 8. I'm definitely an 8'. I said, 'Okay, well we'll come back to that in a little while'.

What I then proceeded to do in that session was not to focus on the fear level straightaway; I would come back and deal with the fears a little later.

Now this wasn't some major moment of inspiration on my part to focus on content first, it was forced on me due to the environment we were in. You see, some of the methods of reducing fear involve some exercises being done out loud, and as we were working in an office environment – although in a private room – there were four glass walls and it just didn't feel like an ideal environment for some of the 'dealing with fear' exercises.

Therefore, I just spent an hour or so with her, getting the content of her presentation right. Looking at what she was thinking of saying and doing and amending and adjusting it . . . what those content changes actually were I will explain later in the book.

After a couple of hours, we got her content right. We got it structured. It was now going to be very easy for her to deliver the content, because of the changes we had made.

We also made it a lot more interesting. Again, I will cover how to make your presentations more interesting a little later.

She then said, 'Wow, that's going to be so exciting to deliver. I'm looking forward to delivering it already, although I'm not sure this particular audience will take me seriously'.

You see, now she knew that audiences in general would enjoy this new version of the presentation after all, she was starting to feel excited about delivering a presentation like this. But she still had concerns about this particular audience liking her or, as she said, taking her seriously.

This meant we also had to deal with what she felt the audience's objections would be to her talking to them on this topic. I cover this later too in the section on dealing with audience objections – and explain how we solved this for her.

At this stage we hadn't done a single thing to do with her confidence, mindset or fear levels. All we had done is to put together some really great content, making it much more interesting and easier to deliver, and sorting out the objections she felt the audience might have about her or the content.

I then said to her, 'So where are you now on a scale of 0 to 10?'

Amazingly, she said, 'I'm a 3 Mark, I'm a 3! I don't think we need to do any more work, Mark. I think I can go and do this!'

Time and time again, I have found that when we get the content right, deal with any objections the person thinks the audience may have about them or their content and get the person to practise, their fear is massively reduced every time they do the presentation or whenever they do any presentation.

So that's why content is really, really important.

But before we get into creating interesting content and dealing with what you think an audience may not like, or may object to, about you or your presentation, let's go through the fear, mindset and confidence side of things.

Now, just like an audience objection, as I write this I have just thought of an objection some readers may have at this point in the book that I need to deal with.

I have just laid out a very strong case for how improving the content and dealing with real or perceived audience objections can make the fear levels fall and the confidence levels can rise, such that dealing with these fear or confidence areas isn't always necessary – or at a minimum can be done after the content is sorted. However, I have also said I am going to cover fears and confidence before I cover content and audience objections!

Here's the thing: especially in a book, some people won't be able to engage with getting into the content while they know they still have this high level of fear or anxiety going on. The difference with what happened to my architect client is that I was there to reassure her that I would come on to help her fears and anxiety once we had the content sorted.

So why mention this other way of dealing with content first at all? Well, to reassure you that even if you still have fear or anxiety once we have been through the mindset and confidence side of things, there is still a huge amount of progress to be made once we have also gone through the content and audience side of things.

This means that if, after the next few chapters, you are still not confident you can do this, you should keep going through the rest of the book until the end. For many people the big progress comes from a combination of the fear reduction/confidence building techniques and the content creation methods.

The Main Steps of the Process

So, here are the main steps.

We are going to look at each of these steps in turn and in detail throughout the book, but first, as an overview, the main steps are:

1. Getting your mindset right: building confidence and reducing fear.
2. Building the motivation, enthusiasm and desire.
3. Being yourself and dealing with mistakes.
4. Having a great 'in-motion' start.
5. Having great content to deliver.
6. Dealing with objections: objections that the audience might have in their mind about you or your topic.

7. Getting the audience to take action.
8. Dealing with difficult audience questions.
9. How to prepare.
10. Delivering on the day.
11. What will being better at presentations mean to you?

We're going to look at each of these in the above order as we move through the book.

PART ONE

The Mindset and Confidence To Present

3
Getting Your Mindset Right: Building Confidence and Reducing Fear

I've already covered the fact that the first stage of this is to be aware of your thinking patterns and mindset and to start thinking about and imagining things going well, not things going badly. Remember my own discovery of how I was thinking very differently about winning business compared to how I was thinking about doing presentations.

You also need to remember that fear massively reduces the more we do things.

We normally experience fear because of uncertainty. And when we say that we lack confidence in doing presentations, that's why we're scared or that's why we've got the fear – due to the uncertainty.

Now, Tony Robbins, the world-famous author and motivational speaker, has a great definition of confidence I once heard him give. He said that confidence is our degree of certainty about an outcome we will get, or how we will perform in a given situation.

When I explore fear or lack of confidence in giving presentations with clients, do you know why they are scared and what they are worried about?

Normally, it's things like:

→ they'll lose their way in the presentation
→ they'll forget their words
→ the audience won't enjoy it
→ they'll make a mistake
→ they'll look stupid
→ they'll freeze
→ they'll mess up.

All these sorts of things go through their minds and many others.

When we talk about belief, confidence, motivation, desire and all those great things, we are really in a word talking about 'mindset'. So, let's take a look at what this mindset is all about.

Recall earlier in the book when I realised years ago that the key difference between something I was really confident at (sales) and something I was really scared of (public speaking) was how I was thinking about it? When I was thinking about going to a sales meeting, I was seeing it all going right. I was thinking things like, 'They're going to love what we do, they're going to love our product, they're going to want to work with us. I can't wait to get there and wow them with what we can do for them'. However, when it came to doing presentations or public speaking, I wasn't thinking about everything going right, I was thinking about everything going wrong!

What if I forget my words? What if I look nervous? What if the audience doesn't enjoy it? What if I pass out? By the time I'd thought all these things, I really didn't feel like doing it. I'd scared myself away from it.

That's why mindset or how we think about things is so important.

As soon as I started to change and think about speaking from the point of view of things going right – and visualised it, imagined it, even pretended that I was doing a great talk – things changed for me. I would practise at home day in, day out, to get that confidence and I'd also go through a number of techniques that I'm going to take you through in this book to do with reducing fear, overcoming hesitation, building confidence, and visualising things going well.

This means, as I said earlier, that I am now able to stand on a stage in front of a thousand people or more, love every single minute of it, not use slides, and just enjoy the moment. Just enjoy it. Look forward to it. Be excited to be there.

As soon as you change your mindset, it changes your results. And I'll explain how as we go through this.

Skill Set/Mindset

Everything we do in life comes down to two aspects: the skill set and the mindset.

Now, a skill set is pretty easy to gain these days. We can go onto the internet, do a quick search, and find the skill set for pretty much anything, because a skill set is:

What you do.
When you do it.
How you do it.

It's all the 'how to' stuff.

But the mindset is very often the missing piece.

The mindset is:

The belief.
The confidence.
The motivation.
Having a compelling goal.

You can have the best skill set in the world, but if you've not got the confidence or the mindset or the belief to get out there and take action, then you're not going to be very successful, happy or confident, nor achieve whatever it is you're looking to achieve.

In my own talks I always use what I think is a great example of mindset.

I'll say to a room of people when presenting on mindset in my own talks:

'Let's say we get a table up here, two phones, two cold calling scripts, and what we're going to do is we're going to get two people out of the audience and we're going to make some cold calls.'

This is where these people are going to come up out of the audience and they're going to pick up a phone and call a business that they do not know and pitch to them on a sale of a product or a service. That's what I tell the audience we are going to do. I'm not actually going to do it in reality, I am just setting the scene for them.

I go on to explain to them that if I was to pick two people out of the audience, and one person picks up the phone and starts dialling – and the other person runs out of the room and doesn't want to do it – what's the difference between these two people?

We all know which of the two people we're more likely to be, and I'll say to them: 'You know, most people are running out of that room'.

Now, why is that?

What's the difference between those two people, the one that runs out of the room and the one that picks up the phone?

First off, they both know how to use a phone!

The person running out of the room probably uses a phone every single day to talk to family and friends and people they know, but in the context of making a 'cold sales call', they panic and run away.

So, you see, between these two people with respect to making these phone calls – the one running away and the one picking up the phone and making the call – there can only be one difference.

They've both got the skill set for making phone calls. OK, they may not have the detailed skill set of doing a sales call, but they could both have read about it in detail.

The only difference there can be is how they're thinking about it. Their mindset.

Their mindset is causing them to either engage in the action and get results or to run away.

Many years ago, back when public speaking was my biggest fear, I too could have read any book on presentation tips and techniques (skill set), but I still wouldn't have done it because I didn't have the confidence, I didn't have the right mindset.

To be really successful and confident at anything, we need to develop both our skill set and our mindset as it is the two areas working together that give us amazing results.

The Mindset Process TFAR

Now we all have this very simple process running in our minds – we have thoughts. We think things on a daily basis. They say we have about 60 000 thoughts a day. I don't know how they work that out, sounds like a lot to me, but apparently it's true.

When we have these thoughts, they change how we feel, whether we feel good and confident or scared and worried. How we feel then determines the action we take or the action we don't take; and the action we take or don't take, of course, determines the results we get.

So that is: Thoughts → Feelings → Action (Or No Action) → Results

Or TFAR as I like to call it.

Now, of course, there are many different sources of personal development and improvement information out there – psychology and all of those sorts of things – and some of these will say that actually the feeling happens first at a subconscious level, and then that spurs off the thoughts. That feeling, though, is coming from an inbuilt subconscious thought triggering the feeling – which then, once we notice it, starts a stream of conscious thoughts.

Whatever the case, it doesn't change the fact that once that initial bad feeling or thought occurs, we perpetuate it with more negative thoughts; sometimes different ones and sometimes the same one or two negative thoughts over and over again.

Then, no matter how the thoughts were originally triggered, we consciously start thinking more and more about all the things that could go wrong.

So, for instance, if an opportunity came up to do a presentation, or to speak in public, back when I had fears, at some subconscious level the fear came up. Once that fear had come up, I then made it a lot worse by thinking through on a conscious level things like, 'Oh, they might not like it, I might forget my words, or I might look nervous, I might pass out'.

I had the opportunity in that moment to notice these thoughts and not be dragged further into them; to stop myself and say:

'Hey, why am I doing this to myself? What else could I be thinking in this situation? What could I do to reduce those concerns? What is it I could do?'

Because, as soft as it may sound, most of the outcomes we get in life are based purely on how we think about things beforehand.

Let me give you a great example: let's say a very shy person is invited to a party on a Saturday night. He doesn't want to go. He hates parties. All week he's thinking:

> 'I don't want to go to this party. I hate parties, but I've got to go because it's my best friend's 21st birthday. But I hate parties, I bet I'll end up standing on my own in the corner with nobody talking to me.'

So, these are his thoughts. Because he is thinking like this, obviously he feels pretty bad about the prospect of going to this party – who wouldn't! All week he's dreading it, he's running these thoughts through his mind every time he thinks about the party, and he's feeling really bad about it.

When he gets there on the Saturday night and he knocks on the door to go in, he thinks he's going into a dreadful situation and, because of that, it's more likely that he'll look down, he'll avoid eye contact with people, he'll stand on his own in the corner – and people will think that he doesn't want to be disturbed, or that he is unapproachable or keeping himself to himself and they won't talk to him. He'll come out at the end of the night and say to himself: 'Wow, I was right, everyone was horrible, I hate parties, no one ever talks to me. I am never going again'.

Now a confident person, on the other hand, he's invited to a party and he thinks very different thoughts, something like – 'Do you know what? I've had a busy few weeks. I can't wait to get out on Saturday night, have some fun, have a few beers, meet some new people. I'm going to have a right laugh!' And he's thinking about it like this all week.

The thoughts he's having about going to this party are causing him to feel really excited and look forward to it. Even during the days before, he may be at work doing a mundane or boring task and every now and then he thinks about how great it will be at the weekend, going to the party.

So, when Saturday comes and he knocks on the door, when he gets there, he thinks he's going into a brilliant situation and therefore he's more likely to keep his head up high, smile, make eye contact with people and acknowledge them.

People will start talking to him, he gets into conversations, and he then comes out at the end of the night saying: 'That was brilliant! What a load of great people I met! That was a fantastic party! I love parties, they're fun!'

The thing is, they've both been to the same party! The same party with the same people, both the shy person and the confident person. But they've had a very different outcome based purely on how they were thinking about it beforehand; based purely on their mindset.

This is how we create a lot of the results and experiences we have in life – based purely on how we think about things before we do them.

Now, of course, we can change our mindset with tools and techniques that I'll cover in this book; by practice and experience, as well as developing skills and doing things a number of times while noticing the progress we are making along the way.

I'm going to talk about all of those different aspects as we go through this, but what I always want to talk about is the subject of confidence, because a lot people will say, 'I'm not confident!'

The first thing we need to do is stop saying that and say, 'I'm not *yet* confident in this particular situation', because as soon as we label ourselves with 'I'm not confident!', it affects our mind in all areas and damages our self-esteem.

I don't care if you're not confident in 50 situations, there are things in your life that you're confident about. There are things in your life that you're certain about. Even if you're certain that you don't have much confidence – you're certain about that, you're confident about that!

But please stop saying 'I'm not confident' and start saying, when something happens, 'Well I'm not confident at doing presentations *yet*, I'm not confident about public speaking *yet*'.

Notice this isn't just about getting specific and making a state-ment about a particular area, it also brings in one of the most powerful words for change – 'Yet'. The word 'yet' says this lack of confidence isn't forever and it assumes that you will change this and become confident. 'Yet' starts to retrain your mind by allow-ing you to start to believe that things will change in the future.

Don't say, 'I'm not confident'. Don't label your whole self as not being confident, because it is only when you understand the specific areas in which you lack confidence that you can start to ask yourself some powerful questions:

'Well, what do I need to do to fix this?'
'What mindset changes do I need?'
'What skill sets do I need to develop?'

'Where do I need to practise?'

'Where do I need to focus my efforts?'

All of the time you're saying, to yourself or others, 'Well, I'm just not confident', it suggests the task is too big because it applies to the whole you and isn't aimed at a specific skill or area of life. This is wrong, and it prevents you from making progress.

Earlier I mentioned that I love what Tony Robbins said once about confidence, that confidence is your degree of certainty about how you'll perform or the outcome you'll get in a given situation.

As soon as you realise that when you say, for example, 'Well I'm not confident at public speaking', that's purely down to your degree of certainty about either the outcome you'll get from doing a talk or how you'll perform in that situation, you then realise:

'Well, hey, I've got a few things here I can look at! I can look at the outcome and why I'm concerned about that and I can also look at how I'll perform. How can I develop my skill set and mindset further in these areas?'

Once we have hope that change is possible, we start to build belief and become prepared to start taking action to change things.

Four Stages of Learning

When looking to make changes to your mindset or skill set you need to be mindful of the four stages of learning, those stages that we all go through when learning or developing a new skill.

(continued)

Understanding them will really help you stop giving up too soon and overreacting to a fear of failure. You will understand that, actually, you're still only partway through the four stages, so you can't yet make that decision that you're no good at something or you're never going to be able to do it.

Stage 1: Unconscious Incompetence

The first stage is called 'unconscious incompetence'.

This is where you are not even aware that a skill exists, and if you were aware that it existed, you wouldn't be able to do it. The best thing to do, as I go through these stages, is to give you an example.

Let's use the example of driving a car or learning to drive a car. When you are, say, six, seven months old, the subject or skill of learning to drive a car isn't known to you. At that young age, you have got what is called unconscious incompetence. That means that you are not aware that the skill exists, and even if you were aware of the skill existing, you wouldn't be able to do it.

Stage 2: Conscious Incompetence

The next stage you get to is 'conscious incompetence'.

This is where you're aware the skill exists, but you know you can't do it.

So, this might be when you're four, five, six years old, or something like that; you can see your parents driving, and you can see that they are doing something to drive a car so you are conscious that a skill of driving a car exists, but you know that you can't do it. You know that your parents have told you there's a thing called driving lessons and driving tests, and so you know you can't do it. You're consciously aware of the skill, but you're incompetent in that you can't do it because you haven't got that skill or ability.

Now this is the stage that most adults are at with pretty much everything in life that they say they 'can't do'. We know that other skills exist, but we also know that we can't do them when it's something new to us, of course. So that's the conscious incompetence stage.

As you're reading this book, you are at least at this stage – the second stage of learning. You are consciously aware that there's a skill or an ability to do great presentations and public speaking, but you probably don't feel you are fully competent at doing it (yet), not fully skilled at doing it, and so you're at the stage of conscious incompetence.

Stage 3: Conscious Competence

The next stage we move on to is when we start to learn and develop a skill – we eventually get to 'conscious competence'.

This is where we can do the skill to some degree, but it's a lot of hard work.

Thinking-wise it's a lot of hard work, and we don't necessarily get the results we'd really like, at least not straight away.

(continued)

Now, back on the driving example again, this is when you're doing your driving lessons. For those of you who've learned to drive, you'll know in those first few lessons – or lessons four, five, six – that you can start to get the car to go along the road, but it's a lot of effort.

You have to think about everything: mirrors, signals, gears, you're probably sweating buckets, you're scared, you're nervous, the car's jumping, especially if it is a manual transmission.

I know when I was learning to drive. I was thinking, 'I'm never going to remember all of this. I'm never going to be able to do this. How do other people do this? This is immense, there's so much to remember, there's so much to learn. I've got to look in the mirror. I've got to do this clutch, and I've got to move this stick, and I've got to put this accelerator down, and bring the clutch up at the same time, and when I come to a stop I've got to put the brake down, and just before I stop I've got to put this clutch down. Wow, so much, how will I ever remember all this?'

This is conscious competence.

Stage 4: Unconscious Competence

Then of course, after a lot of practice the more skill set we develop, the more confidence we get – and one day it clicks and all of a sudden you move from conscious competence to what we call unconscious competence.

This is where you're doing things much more on autopilot.

This is where you're driving down the road after you've

passed your test, you're talking to your friends on the phone hands-free. You may be drinking your coffee, which you shouldn't do when you're driving, by the way, and you get home and think, 'Did I look at those traffic lights at the major junction? I don't remember looking when I turned that corner. I don't remember looking at that crossing, lucky I didn't hit anything'. But you were on autopilot. You were displaying unconscious competence.

You see, conscious competence with public speaking would be when you know you're still developing the skill, and you're going out and you're thinking in a more positive way before you start a presentation. And then you're doing it and you're getting some results – and you're building on that. You still have to pay close attention though to everything you are doing.

Until one day it clicks and you move into the final stage – 'unconscious competence' – where you're just having experiences and saying things like:

> 'Hey, I just did that presentation and it went brilliantly. I even made a couple of slip ups, but in the moment I just bounced off them, the audience laughed and, if anything, it made it even better. That was something I would never have done in the past. Wow, I've made a lot of progress.'

So remember: there are four stages to learning, and if you're not yet getting the results you're looking for, things aren't yet working out for you, it only means

(continued)

37

you're not all the way through the four stages yet. As with everything, it's always about being curious about the results you're getting, doing more of what works, less of what doesn't work, developing your skill set further and developing your mindset.

For most things in life, if other people are out there doing it and getting results, especially with things like public speaking, there must be a way to do it. They've just developed the skill set and mindset needed to do it, and you can develop that skill set and mindset too.

That's what it's all about in this book, of course. Developing both the skill set and mindset to deliver fantastic presentations with confidence.

Fear of Failure

In this section, we are going to explore the very common area known as fear of failure.

I find that with most people I have helped, fear of failure – or the fear of not getting the outcome they're looking for – holds them back from taking any action in the first place. Hence, they are actually doomed to guaranteed failure because you can't usually achieve anything by not taking any action at all.

This is also the case when dealing with public speaking and presentations. After all, I haven't met anyone who is scared it's going to go well! They are all scared it's going to go wrong one way or another. They are scared that they are going to fail and not get at least a reasonable outcome, typically the minimum that they would be looking for in that situation.

Now, you may remember earlier in the book, when I was talking about mindset, I used the example of two people cold-calling. One picks up the phone and makes the call, while the other one runs out of the room and doesn't want to make a call.

Do you remember what the difference was between the two people?

I highlighted the point that there can only be one real difference: how they're thinking about it, their mindset, especially at that initial stage of taking the action to pick up the phone. After all some people, even with no skill set knowledge, would have 'given it a go to see what happened' due to their own mindset.

So, given that fear of failure is one of the biggest things that holds people back, here is how I like to think of things, especially public speaking for instance, or doing presentations: that there's only two possible outcomes.

It either goes really, really, well; or you've got a funny story to tell people later, coupled with a learning experience for next time.

You know, when things go wrong, one of the best things we can do is see the funny side of it. Go and tell five other people about what happened and relay it as a funny experience. Because, by the time we've told five other people, we don't take it so seriously ourselves.

As an example, if you went to start a conversation with someone at an event, and they ignored you, there are many meanings that could be attached to this outcome. For instance, you don't know that they actually ignored you. They may not have heard you. They may not have understood you. They may not have thought that you were talking to them. They may be really shy and lack confidence. And countless other reasons. So, you don't know that they actually ignored you, but let's say that you thought they had.

Now, you could cringe in the moment, go away thinking, 'Oh, I must never do that again, just go up to someone I don't know and attempt to start a conversation', or you could think, 'Oh, that was really interesting and funny'. And, when you see a friend later, or family member, say something like 'Hey, you'll never guess what happened to me. I was standing next to this person, something had happened, and I just said something to them about it, and they completely ignored me! I wish the ground could have opened up and swallowed me in the moment. How embarrassing was that?'

Now, by the time you have told five different people, in an upbeat way, that it was a funny experience, you will not take that situation seriously at all. You will have embedded it in your mind differently and you will see it differently. This event in your mind will now have humour attached to it rather than fear and hence change how you think about it and your ability to take action again in the future.

So, with a positive or growth mindset, there are only two possible outcomes: it went really well, or it's a funny story to tell someone.

I know many years ago, when I started my own journey of looking to change my confidence in talking to people, not on stage but out in public in general, something happened where I used this way of looking at things.

I was walking to a meeting and, as I did so, I passed this store. Outside this store was a little dog, tied up, its lead was tied up to a post.

There was an elderly couple next to this dog. This particular dog looked like the sort of dog that my wife and I were thinking that we might get. We had been discussing that we might get a Cocker Spaniel, and there one was. Well, I thought it was a Cocker Spaniel.

As I walked past, I had one of those moments where I thought about asking them if their dog was a Cocker Spaniel but then hesitation came in, and I didn't do it. But I got about three or four steps further and said to myself, 'No, no, no, Mark. This is stupid. Go do it'.

So, I turned around, and I said to them, 'Oh, excuse me, Is that a Cocker Spaniel? Because my wife and I were thinking of getting one, so I just wondered if that was a Cocker Spaniel'.

One of them said, 'It's not our dog, dear'!

So, in that moment, I could have gone, 'Oh my god, how stupid do I feel? How ridiculous am I? I must never, ever ask people things again, because I end up looking really stupid and really humiliated'.

But, instead, what I did was, I said, 'That's a funny story'. I wouldn't have said anything to those people in the past. I'd done a lot of changing at this point, but I said, 'That's a funny story'.

And as soon as I saw my first friend, and then when I got to my meeting, and when I spoke to other people later that day, I said, 'You'll never guess what happened to me today. I was walking down the street. I saw this dog. I said to this elderly couple next to the dog, "Hey, is that a Cocker Spaniel," and they said, "It's not our dog". Can you believe how stupid I felt? Can you believe how ridiculous I felt in that moment?'

It became a funny story, and it's not something that plagues me thinking back – 'Oh, my God! Can you remember that time I spoke all those years ago to those people? I felt like such an idiot!' – no! It's a funny story! It made me laugh and it was something to share with others. You see, Napoleon Hill, in his famous book, *Think and Grow Rich*, said that failure is really just an unplanned outcome, and that we don't fail at anything in life until we decide to give up going for it.

For example, if I set myself the goal that I want to get five new clients, and I had five meetings with potential clients and they all said 'No', I haven't failed, because the possibility of me getting five new clients still exists. I have just had five unplanned outcomes.

Now, after five people have said 'No' to me, I might want to take some feedback and think, 'Am I saying the right things? Am I meeting with the right people? Am I doing the right things?'; but I haven't failed. I fail when I say 'That's it, I'm giving up. I'm not doing this anymore. I'm obviously no good at doing this. I'm giving up'.

That's when I really fail, when I give up. Failure for most things in life is in our control when we adopt a positive or growth mindset.

Four-Year-Old Children

Now, we can also learn a lot from four-year-olds.

When my son, James, was four years old, we got him one of those little Nintendo DS games, the computer games the kids love to play on. Do you think, at four years old, he can read the manual that is in 20 languages, over 64 pages on how to play that game?

No, he can't read one language that well at that age. So, what does he do? He plays around with it. He tries different things. He pushes different buttons. He sees he's making progress and thinks: 'Well, I'll do more of that'. His little man dies, or he loses the race, he thinks: 'Oh, I won't do that again'. He continues to do more of what works, less of what doesn't work, until he can play that game perfectly and win nearly every single time. But that's what we, as adults, won't do most of the time.

Like when a child gives us one of those games and says: 'Nan, Grandad, Mum, Dad, Brother, Sister, whatever, have a go at my game'. Most of us have a go, die in the game or lose the race instantly and announce 'Load of rubbish! Don't know why you waste your time with those stupid games!'

Why is that?

Most people don't like it to be seen that they can't do things perfectly the first time they do them.

For some weird reason, somewhere along the line we have forgotten that there's a learning curve to everything we do in life. We expect to be an expert straight away, and if we're not an expert straight away, we're obviously no good, we're obviously never going to do it.

We forget that we need to develop the skill set. We also need to develop mindset, belief, confidence and motivation, and then we will be able to do more of those things.

Do you not think if you spent as many hours as a young child does on those games, that you'd be able to play them really well? Of course, you would.

So, we need to be more like a four-year-old from time to time. Be curious about the results we're getting. I mean, after all, what does a four-year-old do? They live in the moment, they don't give a damn what anyone else thinks, and they keep going at things until they get the result they're after! How much more successful or happy would we be in life, work, careers, business or relationships if we adopted the mindset of a four-year-old from time to time?

So, the good news is, and I've never been proven wrong on this before – and I don't think I'm going to be proven wrong by anyone reading this – we were all once four-year-olds!

We've all got that mindset in us. All that's happened is that, since we were four years old, we've learned a lot of things that have held us back. We've worried too much about failing, about what other people think, or about embarrassing ourselves.

We need to unlearn that way of thinking, and get back to the mindset of a four-year-old, and start behaving like a four-year-old, because we were all four years old once and we all had that mindset that anything is possible, when we were younger.

So, instead of getting down and upset or angry when some-thing to do with public speaking or presentations doesn't go too well, adopt the four-year-old mindset and instead be curious about the result that happened and think about what you could do differently next time.

Thoughts, Beliefs and 'I Can't Do Presentations'

As already mentioned, your thoughts – whatever you think – generate your feelings or your emotional state, which in turn determine the quality of action that you take or whether you take any action at all (because a lot of the time when fear comes up we don't take any action), and that in turn deter-mines the outcome or your results.

Now, when you have good thoughts about doing some-thing, you get good feelings, confident feelings, empowering feelings – whatever is appropriate to the thoughts – and you take more effective action and you get better results. And, when you get good results, you are going to have more good thoughts based on how well you did, and it's going to go on and on like a self-fulfilling prophecy – and then you are in what's often called the 'zone' where everything seems to go right for you.

I'm sure at some time you have experienced an occasion when everything seems to be going right and you are in the zone.

The trouble with this formula or mechanism is if you think bad thoughts you get bad feelings and a bad emotional state, bad quality of action (or no action), bad outcome and results.

So, if we could all instantly switch and say 'right, from now on I'm just thinking good thoughts' we would be fixed; but, unfortunately, there's this subconscious part of the brain that's running on autopilot which is involved, and so we humans usually struggle to do this.

The alternative, then, is to apply tools and techniques to our way of thinking, or our fears that hold us back in certain situations, and this is what we've been looking at so far in this book.

Now it's time to look into this a bit deeper; so, yes, it is about thoughts but it's also actually more than that – at the end of the day it is really all about the emotions that those thoughts cause.

Most decisions you ever make in life are emotional decisions somewhere along the line.

Not only that, so are everyone else's!

So, the thoughts we make other people think by our words and actions are of huge importance, because they influence their decisions and the actions they take. This is why public speaking and doing presentations is such a fantastic thing to do and such a great skill to develop, because you are able to influence the thoughts and emotions of the audience by the words you speak and how you say them.

For most of us, we have a lot of thoughts about the things we know would help take our success to the next level, such as public speaking, but we suffer from what I call the 'I can't' virus, which is where we tell ourselves we can't do it.

Time and time again I hear people say 'I can't do talks or presentations' or 'I can't speak in public'. Those are actually limiting beliefs and there are some easy exercises to work through to start to change how you feel about the things you tell yourself you 'can't do' that are related to public speaking, talks and presentations.

The 'I can't virus'

First, you need to decide which limiting belief or fear it is that you want to work on related to public speaking or giving presentations. The process that follows will help you to discover what this is.

Task 1

So, go ahead and pick something where you say:

'I can't . . .'.

For example:

'I can't speak in public'.

Or

'I can't do talks or presentations'.

Whatever it is, decide what you would like to work on first – usually this would be your biggest 'I can't' statement in terms of holding you back or causing doubts about your abilities.

(continued)

Now, you have to realise that for most things in life where you say:

'I can't'

it usually means

'I won't because . . .'

and what follows the 'because' is some fear or imagined consequence.

When we start looking at 'I can't' there are some important questions we can ask ourselves to start to break down that limiting belief.

With each of these questions, I urge you not just to think about it, but to write down as many of the ideas and thoughts that come to you for each question as you can. No matter how silly the thought might be, don't dismiss it because the chances are it is affecting how you feel about doing presentations or public speaking on some level.

Task 2

Then, the next question to ask yourself is this:

'How do you know you can't?'

This question is asking you to think about what makes you believe that you can't do this particular thing. You see, we are often too quick to say we 'can't' and believe it and do not allow ourselves to break down and analyse what really makes up that belief or fear.

This is what usually happens when I ask this same question to people directly:

ME: 'How do you know you can't?'

They respond with the answer:

'I just can't'.

When I ask again and insist on an answer they usually go to one of two positions:

1. 'I have never done it before' – which of course does not mean they 'can't'. It is just something they have not yet learnt and practised.

Or, the most common response they give is:

2. 'I did it once and it went badly' – well in this case it certainly does not mean they 'can't', they have actually done it at least once! It just means they did not get the result they hoped for.

Now, if you've attempted something and did not get the desired result, or you've never done presentations in public before, you need to understand that while you may need some skill set training, motivation or belief, it certainly doesn't mean you can't do it ever!

This is about realising how things might be possible – what would have to happen for it to be possible for you – and is the first step in thinking about why you say you 'can't', because as you begin to understand this, you can then do something about it.

(continued)

Think about this question and write the answer down. Remember, the question is:

'How do you know you can't do presentations or speak in public?'

Now, as long as you've done the above and are not cheating, we can move on to examine this 'I can't' claim a bit further.

With the above you have explored the evidence and reasons why you say you can't do this yet through the question of 'How do you know you can't?' I hope you didn't stall on 'I just can't' – that's a popular first response, but ask yourself again 'How do you know you can't?' and get that answer revealed; stay calm, relax and ponder it and let your ideas just come up.

OK, so now, if you have done that, you are ready for the next step . . .

Task 3

The next question to take this even further is to ask:

'What specifically prevents me doing presentations or public speaking?'

This starts your mind thinking about your fears, imagined consequences of what might happen if you did attempt it, and all the sort of things you typically think about and worry about that might or might not happen if you were to do this.

So, once again, think about it and take your time, list on a piece of paper everything that comes to mind, no matter how insignificant it might seem.

List all the reasons and thoughts and internal comments that come up when you ask 'What specifically prevents me doing this?' – replacing of course the words 'doing this' with whatever it is you are changing – for example 'What specifically prevents me doing presentations or public speaking?'

Once you have done this we can move to the next stage.

Task 4

So, previously we asked:

'What specifically prevents me doing this?' and started your mind thinking about your fears and consequences.

This next step is a little easier in that all I want you to do is think about this fear or limiting belief and the fact you can't do it, and say to yourself:

'It's not that I can't do it, it's that I won't do it'.

Do this several times throughout the day; start to convince yourself that it is basically under your control, that you are the one who is deciding you can't.

Some people suggest you think of it being under your control by saying something like:

'I can engage in the act of not . . .' followed by the activity or thing you fear doing.

(continued)

For example, 'I can engage in the act of not speaking in public'.

This may sound weird, but you will notice the internal feelings or tug associated with this statement is a little (or a lot) different to how it feels when you simply say 'I can't . . .'.

So, once again, think about it, ponder it and write your thoughts and answers down.

A quick recap of what we have done in this section so far:

You have asked for the evidence that causes you to say you can't do something by asking yourself:

'How do I know I can't do this?'

We then looked at the fears and consequences you currently associate with doing the thing you fear by asking yourself:

'What specifically prevents me?'

Then we moved to understanding we are ourselves in fact deciding we 'can't' and that it is actually under our control – realising it's usually that we 'won't' do things as opposed to we 'can't' do them.

Task 5

Now I want you to make a list of all the positives to your life if you were to be able to do the thing you say you can't do, i.e. speak in public or do presentations.

Remember, this is the positives. How would it make your life better if you could do this with ease?

For example, things like:

I'd be more successful.
I'd be able to help a lot of people.
I'd be really proud of myself.
I'd earn more money.
I'd have more opportunities.
I'd be able to realise my true potential.
I'd be able to do the things I want to do for my family.

It's important that this is in your own words and you write them all down and feel good about them.

As we are working through this, you are probably already starting to think about public speaking and presentations in a slightly different way. And now you have made a list of all the positives to your life if you were to be able to do the thing you say you can't currently do related to public speaking.

Task 6

Next, we are going to look at it from the other side.

So now make a list of all the negatives to your life if you never overcome this and are never able to do presentations or speak in public.

Remember this is the negatives of never overcoming this, so it could be things like:

I won't be as successful as I could be.
I will always regret not being able to do this.

(continued)

I won't be able to do all the things I want for my family.

I'll never know just how good my life could have been.

It's important again that it's in your words and you write them down.

Most people already ask these questions of themselves. But they do it the wrong way round – they come up with all the positives of not doing it and the negatives of doing it, and that is how they motivate themselves away from ever overcoming their fears associated with public speaking and presentations.

With the previous two questions, you have analysed the positives to your life if you overcame the fear and the negatives of not ever overcoming it. In life we either motivate ourselves towards good things or away from bad things. What method we use is based on our own way of using our mind and the context of our life it relates to. For example, let's say we have two people both in the situation of having less than ideal (for them) finances and both wanting to be very wealthy.

Now one of them may motivate themselves to do something about it by thinking on a regular basis about how good it will feel when they are wealthy, what they would do, how great their life would be. The other person may motivate themselves by thinking about getting away from the bad situation they are currently in and what will happen if things don't improve – will they lose everything, what other people will think, etc.

The first person is motivated towards the positive future desired outcome; the second is motivated away from the current negative situation and how bad it could get in the future if they don't change things.

Both can work as motivation strategies, although whenever you are motivating yourself to avoid negative outcomes it tends to keep you feeling bad and can make you seem a very down or distant person to others around you, which isn't ideal if part of your solution involves getting others on board with something or agreeing with you. For that to happen both parties tend to need to be enthusiastic and positive.

Task 7

Now, in the last two questions you have been looking at the positives of overcoming the fears and negatives of not overcoming them.

Now read the positive list and negative list and see which one makes you feel more driven to overcome the fear; is it the thought of all the positives you'd gain, or is it the thought of all the negatives you want to avoid?

It's important that between reading and thinking about each list you take a break and go and do something else, then come back in a calm, neutral state to review the other list and see how you feel.

(continued)

You can repeat the process a number of times, but it is essential you take this break between reading each list and pondering what it means and how it feels, otherwise the emotions generated from reading one list can contaminate the feelings about the other list. For example, if you have just read the negative list and it has made you feel really bad, and then start reading the positive list, then you may not feel much better as you are still down from the negative list and the effect it had on you.

For many of you there will be a difference; a few may feel the same and be equal in the amount of motivation each list gives them.

When you know which list motivates you the most, I want you to start thinking about that list in your mind several times today and really get the understanding of how important it is to you to overcome this.

We will do anything in life if we have a good enough reason!

If you have equal drive from both lists, then I suggest that you go with the positives.

Summary

Let's do a summary of what we have done with our initial 'I can't' situation and add some more thoughts to it.

You have been thinking about your fear or limiting belief in a different way, and rather than just saying and accepting you can't do something, you have actually taken the time to realise just how much it would mean to you to overcome this.

With all the understanding and knowledge you have gained about your fear, the evidence and the consequences, I want you to really think about how good it will feel with this fear gone. How great life will be when you are able to speak in public and deliver presentations that your audience love – and you enjoy giving.

The best way to do this is by using techniques such as affirmations, visualisation and anchoring that we will cover in the next chapter once we have finished off a few more areas of fear and other things that hold people back from public speaking.

Another way to look at beliefs that may hold you back

Now, another way to look at beliefs is to look at the area of life where you are not taking the actions you would like to take or feeling the way you'd like to feel and check in with yourself and see what belief might be holding you back.

For example, let's say someone doesn't like doing presentations, but they don't know what the exact belief is that is holding them back in order to work on it.

What they can do to find out the belief that is likely to be holding them back is to ask themselves this question:

'In order to feel like this or act like this in this situation what must I believe about myself, about others and the world in general?'

You'll be surprised how new ideas and thoughts can spring to mind when you ask better questions of yourself. Too often we say 'Why can't I do this?' and answer ourselves in a way that is not very helpful.

So, apply this method of discovering hidden or unknown beliefs to anything related to public speaking that you want to work on. Or, what would be even better is to notice over the next few days any bad emotions or feelings, anything you think or feel that's holding you back, and simply say to yourself:

'In order to feel like this or act like this in this situation what must I believe about myself, about others and the world in general?'

Maybe you could apply the above to a time in the past when you avoided giving a presentation or had a lot of fear about giving one.

One of the things I'd really like you to do is become more aware of the feeling you get when fears come up or negative emotions emerge – perhaps even when you get annoyed if something is not going your way.

Notice these times and ask yourself the above question.

Often, we are so familiar with our day-to-day emotions that, although we feel them, we just accept them – they have always been there and 'it's just how things are'. No, it is how things have been and you can change that.

You can be excited about the things you once feared and that will inspire you to take action, coupled with enthusiasm, and then go onto get great results.

If we take time to notice our beliefs and feelings and pay attention to them, and ask ourselves the above questions, then we become more aware of how we work.

Once you know how something works it is so much easier to improve it or change it.

The Fear Release Process

One of the big things we have been looking at with mindset and everything covered so far is reducing fear.

There are a number of ways to reduce fear.

One way is getting out there and doing it, just doing the thing you fear – such as public speaking. Eventually you'll get used to it and you'll realise that you do survive and there's nothing really to be afraid of.

Another way is to look at the beliefs behind our fears, what holds us back, what are the reasons for this fear – and we did that in the previous sections of this chapter.

We also looked at the benefits of getting out there and doing presentations and public speaking, what it would mean to your life – because, sometimes, we'll push through and do things if we can see there's a big enough reason or a big enough benefit.

Another way is to reduce the fear feeling itself. So, what we're looking at specifically in this section is working directly on that feeling of fear or emotion.

When you reduce the fear of public speaking, and increase the desire to do it, you'll be better placed to push through and you'll start taking the actions needed and getting the results you desire.

The other way, then, is to look to release that fear energy. I've covered this in more detail in my book *How to Talk to Absolutely Anyone*, but this is how it works at a basic level.

When we're in a fear situation, we experience fear on a physical level. We get a feeling in our stomach or our chest, it will sometimes rise up inside us and spread around our body, or it will churn around in our stomachs; some feelings or sensations like this will go on internally when we're really, really scared. We will actually feel the fear on an intense internal level.

Now, one of the really good ways of reducing fear is to start to become conscious and aware when that fear feeling happens, when it comes up.

So, you may have a situation where someone mentions to you that you may need to do a presentation, and you start to feel the fear come up. Now, you don't have to wait for this to happen in real life; most people can imagine the situation occurring and start to feel the fear even though they are not in the situation. For example, people with a fear of spiders often start to panic and squirm if you talk about spiders, even though there isn't one in the room!

So, when you notice that dreaded fear feeling come up, just notice it, don't get dragged into it.

Because what often happens when we fear something, is that we will start thinking about that thing, overthinking it, running it through, thinking about the disasters that could happen – creating more and more fear. So it self-perpetuates and gains power and momentum through the things we are saying in our heads and through our inner voice when we're talking to ourselves – and the feelings we generate are the same or very similar to the sort of scenes we imagine when faced with the situation in real life.

So, the emotional fear feeling that starts is fuelled by the ongoing thoughts we have and becomes an endless cycle.

Therefore, what you want to do as a first step is to just notice the fear feeling when it comes up, that uncomfortable feeling.

Just focus on it; stop the internal chatter. Don't start thinking about the situation; just observe and notice the physical feeling.

Just say something casual to yourself like 'There it is', and imagine it dissolving away. The important thing is to not start thinking about the situation or fear but focus only on the feeling as a sensation in your body.

Some people imagine that there is a funnel that's taking it away out of them.

Other people visualise and imagine it floating away like a cloud passing by.

Whatever works for you; but the key is that when you feel that fear feeling coming up, don't get dragged into it and start dramatising it in your head. Just observe it and say something curious like 'Oh, there it goes again. There's that fear feeling', in an almost dismissive way, as a sort of curiosity. And then focus on the feeling, feel what it feels like, and you'll notice that it will gradually start to disburse.

Eckhart Tolle covers this area of fear release quite a lot in his work.

The more you do this over time, the better you get at it. And the better you get at it, the quicker the results are.

But it's just another way of reducing that fear feeling when it comes up.

So, notice it for what it is. It is just a feeling based on your old way of thinking. It isn't real.

You see, unfortunately, what normally happens to us is that the prehistoric part of our brain becomes engaged when fear comes up in a situation, and it can trigger the 'fight or flight' mechanism – so the prehistoric part of your brain is saying 'If I attempt to do a talk and it goes wrong, or I say something wrong then I will look stupid and I will die!' That's what your prehistoric brain is likely saying to you on a subconscious level – it goes to an irrational level of subconscious thinking.

But rationally, on a conscious level, we know that that's absurd. We know that that is not a rational thought process.

So a lot of the time, in most daily situations, when that fear comes up it's an irrational reaction to something that isn't that bad or hasn't happened yet and may not happen.

Those times when you consciously know that this isn't a real life or death situation, you want to notice the fear coming up and observe it. But don't get dragged into it. And as for that inner voice going on in your head, make sure that more and more you are changing it into being an inner coach rather than an inner critic.

So, that's a voice that's saying: 'Yes, you can do this. Of course you can do this'. 'I can see other people doing talks and presentations with ease and soon I will be able to do that too'. That's a positive inner coach voice. What most people have, most of the time, is an inner critic internal voice: 'Oh, they won't like it if I do that. I'll probably fumble on my words. I'll probably sound nervous'. You've got to change that and adopt that more positive inner voice.

So, play with it today. Take a 0-10 SUD scale reading. Get a fear level by thinking about an aspect of public speaking that currently scares you.

Go back through the previous scenarios. Look at what your SUD level is on each of those. Try the release method. Search online for the Sedona method, or Energy Release method. There's a lot of free material on this and you can learn and practise a technique that will start to reduce that fear level when you think about a certain situation.

All you have to do is imagine yourself in a situation. See what you'd see. Hear what you'd hear. Really imagine what it would be like and then close your eyes if that makes it easier for you. But what you want to then do is, as soon as you start to feel that uncomfortable feeling – whether it's very subtle or it's very intense, do that release exercise and observe it without being pulled into it.

An important point here is that different techniques work for different people and you don't need every technique to work for you. Some people experience change with just one technique, others may get some improvement and then find another technique helps them the rest of the way.

4
Building the Motivation, Enthusiasm and Desire

Anchoring

In this section we will talk about anchors. Before we get into exploring how to use them, I want to explain why we are looking at them.

Anchors are a way of making you feel good in the moment, a way of quickly shifting your emotions so you can feel excited, confident and positive at the flick of a switch.

This is very useful and can be done very discreetly to enable you to get a quick confidence boost when needed; for example, before getting up to do a talk or presentation.

They can also be used to add the all-important feeling element to affirmations and visualisations, which we are covering later in this chapter.

So, what is an anchor?

Well, an anchor in the personal development sense that we're looking at in this section, is something that triggers an emotional response in you. Anchors are commonplace. You've got them, they happen all the time. It's when something happens in the external environment: somebody says something, you hear something, you see something, you taste something, you smell something. It triggers a memory that results in a feeling.

The reason we are looking at this technique is that it is a way for you to change from feeling uncertain to feeling confident in seconds. Now, wouldn't that be useful just before a presentation?

A few great examples you'll easily relate to: there are certain songs that when they come on you feel uplifted and like you could take on the world, like you could do absolutely anything. That's an anchor. That piece of music has caused an emotional reaction in you. Another anchor might be a piece of music that makes you feel sad, it makes you feel down, it makes you feel tearful. Another anchor: a smell of a perfume or a particular flower that reminds you of someone from your childhood or someone from years ago and you have a feeling – good or bad – about that person.

A classic one is when we go into a school as an adult. We go back into school, perhaps for parents' evening or something for our children, and a lot of us get this overwhelming fear or dread of being back at school like a child again. Why is that? Well for most people what that's about is the smell of the floor polish, or the smells in the school that actually take you right back to when you were there. Smells are powerful.

They go right to the central part of the brain and trigger that emotion very quickly.

So, if things can fire off randomly like this, if we can smell something or hear something and it creates a good or a bad state in us, what if we could make that happen at will? What if we could say: 'Do you know what? I'd love to feel really confident, upbeat, like I could do anything at the moment'.

What if you could make that happen whenever you wanted?

Well, of course, a really easy way to make it happen – although not very practical for a lot of situations – is to have the piece of music that makes you feel like you can do anything on your phone or your music player. And, just before you go into a situation that you want to do well in, you put the headphones in and listen to the music and you get all pumped up and go in there and get your results. You could do that. Of course, it's a bit of fumbling about with getting the headphones on and off and all that, and you might lose your state. It also isn't that discreet in a lot of situations.

What if we could do something a lot more discreet, something that people wouldn't even notice we're doing?

Well, we can. What we can do, because the brain learns really quickly, is teach our brain and our body a connection between a physical gesture and an emotional response. Hence, rather than waiting for the right song or smell to trigger a good emotional feeling, we can use a physical gesture instead.

What a lot of people do to build an anchor in this way is to use their hands. They will do something like squeeze their thumb and first two fingers together, to be the anchor. What they will do to create this anchor is they experience the situation of feeling really confident – perhaps through listening to the piece of music that makes them feel really confident, or imagining a situation going really well – and while they're in that confident state and feeling really, really on top of the world, they will do the gesture; in this example, they would gently squeeze their thumb and first two fingers together.

Just at the point they sense that the confidence state or the upbeat state is about to fade away, they'll let go. And then they'll put the music back on, or imagine the situation again, or the memory of a time when they felt really confident and on top of the world, and as they reach that point of feeling really good, feeling really powerful, put their fingers together again until the point it's about to fade off or drift away – and then let go.

The important thing is you need to do this a number of times so your mind learns that when you squeeze your fingers together it makes you feel like this. It will then happen just with the physical gesture and without the music being there or you thinking about the situation you used to originally create the anchor.

So you do that four or five times and what you'll actually find is – if you then take a step back, walk around for a while, shake yourself down, whatever, and then back to a neutral state – when you do that physical gesture again you'll get the same or a very similar feeling come up.

And what you do is you practise. We call it 'stacking'. You practise stacking the anchor – i.e. experiencing the good state and doing the physical gesture a number of times – until, when you actually do it, you think 'Yes, that feels great. That feels really great'.

It's important that the physical gesture is very similar each time, including the intensity of the squeeze.

You can find a video demonstrating how to do this technique at:

https://www.markrhodes.com/public-speaking-videos

The steps again are:

1. Remember a time you felt really confident or on top of the world, or something so great happened that if you thought about it now you would experience that feeling again. Think about that time. See what you saw at the time in your mind. Hear what you heard at the time. That might be what people were saying or what you were saying to yourself at the time of the original event.

2. When you start to feel really good, make that gesture of squeezing the fingers together. When you're sensing it's about to die off, let go, because what we want to anchor is the feeling building up and feeling good, rather than dying off. The mistake a lot of people make is they keep doing this gesture all the way through the feeling going up and the feeling coming back down at the end. We don't want that. The feeling going up is what we want to experience and anchor. So we make sure we release it at the point where we feel or intuitively know it's going to drop back soon.

(continued)

3. You do that a number of times. You could also put some music on that makes you feel upbeat.

4. Once you've finished building that anchor a number of times, you walk around, shake yourself down or whatever to basically get yourself back into a neutral state so you can do a proper test – and then do it again; feel that good feeling come up.

Of course, you don't have to hold your hand up to do this. When you use your anchor, the best method is to have your hands by your side – and then who's going to see when you walk into a room, or you're about to go and talk to somebody you don't know, and you want to get a boost of confidence and a boost of feel-good energy, that you are discreetly squeezing your thumb and two fingers together?

It could be any gesture though. I have an anchor myself that I've developed, because anchors develop naturally over time. One of my anchors when I go on stage to do a talk is to rub my hands together on the walk up. This puts me in a really upbeat mode, ready to go on and do a great and powerful talk for the audience.

So, start building yourself an anchor, practising with it, and firing it off and using that feeling to make yourself feel really, really good when you need to feel really good.

You're making anchors all of the time – when things happen and you have an emotional reaction – and when that thing happens a couple of times you create an anchor. Someone who has a fear of dogs has created an anchor; it's more than likely that when a dog barks or they see a dog, fear comes up. So they have taught themselves that when that happens, they feel fear.

What we are doing with our created anchor is we're saying that when this happens, I feel great. And that means that you've now got the ability to make yourself feel good and empowered whenever you want to, whenever you need to. It's going to be immensely useful to you as we go through these different situations.

But one word of warning on this is that when you go into a situation, you've got to remember to use it. So many times people forget to. And I'll be covering how to achieve that when we talk about visualising in the next section. So get out there, press your anchors, and see how good you can make yourself feel.

Affirmations

If you've ever looked to make a change in your life – maybe achieve more success, be more confident, get better in social situations, whatever it is – if you've looked into the world of personal development and change, you've come across affirmations.

Affirmations are a great way to build confidence and belief as well as motivation and desire toward becoming a great presenter.

The problem with affirmations is that people see these as just saying the same thing over and over again and some magic happening and everything changing; yet rarely do things improve.

So, the first thing is, do affirmations work?

Yes, they do work. But it's not just about saying the same thing over and over again. There's something else to it and it's the reason why most people cannot get affirmations working for them. I'm now going to share with you how to make affirmations work, where most people go wrong, and how you can avoid those mistakes and have affirmations that really work, are easy to do and change the things in your life you want to change.

We're going to focus your affirmations on becoming great and confident at public speaking and doing presentations; however, you can use these exact same techniques in all areas of your life, now and in the future.

So, as I said, affirmations do work. But most people don't get them to work. Why is that?

The reason is that people seem to think that affirmations are all about coming up with a load of statements that you just say over and over again like you're in detention at school writing lines out.

'I'm getting better and better every day.'
'I'm getting better and better every day.'
'I'm getting better and better every day.'
'I have achieved success.'
'I have achieved success.'
'I have achieved success.'

That is not how affirmations work, and it's the reason most people can't get them to work for them.

The important thing with affirmations is the *feeling that you feel when you say them.* The words are nowhere near as important as the feeling you feel. It's the feeling that sends the signal to your mind, and that's what makes everything change. And I'm going to explain exactly how it works and why it works to you, and I'm also going to prove it to you with real-life examples that many of you reading this will have experienced in your own life already.

So, with affirmations, you have to say them as if you've already achieved the result you are looking for. But why is that?

It is because the important thing is the feeling. And the feeling you need to feel when you say your affirmations is like you're already that person, you're already that confident public speaker, or you're already great at delivering presentations and you look forward to doing them – or whatever it is that your affirmation is about. I'll explain why shortly.

Now you haven't got to say affirmations continually all day long, multiple times. Myself, I say each affirmation three times.

For example, I may be looking to change three or four things at any one time in my own life and so I'll have an affirmation for each of those three or four things. I will say each affirmation three times in the morning at the start of the day, and three times just before I go to sleep at night.

So, if I'm changing four things and they're all being said three times, that's just twelve statements to say (and feel!) in one session.

It doesn't take that long to do, but the important thing is that as you say each one you need to pause, think about it, imagine it and feel how good that feels now as if it is already reality.

You've got to experience what that feels like now.

It's going to be tricky for some people, because people often think, 'Well, I'm not confident at the moment', or 'I'm not a great public speaker'. Well, you've got to practise it.

This is why a lot of times you'll hear people in the self-help or personal development worlds saying that one of the first steps is having gratitude and thinking about the things you are grateful for.

The reason this is often said is, if you get up in the morning and the first thing that you think about, no matter how simple and basic it is, is that you're really grateful for waking up that morning, you're really grateful for your health (if you've got good health), you're really grateful for your family (if you've got a family), whatever it is, whatever small things you can find or big things you can find in your life you're grateful for, then as you think about them and say thank you for them, you feel good.

What this does is it gets that feeling of positivity and being grateful started inside of you.

Now, don't worry because I'm talking about feelings here. I'm going to give you real-world examples of this coming into play as we go through this part of the book.

When you do the gratitude exercises and you're thinking about those things you are grateful for, you are getting that 'already-achieved-it-now feeling' because you have – and are happy about those things you are grateful for. This is the same sort of feeling you want to feel during your affirmations; hence, gratitude gets you in the right feeling state for doing affirmations. It is like an anchor in that we are borrowing feelings generated from gratitude to use in our affirmations we are about to do each day.

Another way to do it is put on some music that makes you feel alive, makes you feel upbeat, makes you feel on top of the world.

Get those good feelings going and that's when you can go into saying your affirmations *in the present tense*, and then you're much more likely to feel comfortable saying them as if you've already achieved them.

That's the thing here, the affirmations have got to be in the present tense. It can't be 'I'm going to feel really fantastic when . . .' because that projects it into the future and the feeling associated with it is different.

Many people make the mistake of doing affirmations like this:

'Oh, it's going to be really great when I have the confidence to speak in public.'
'I'm going to be really successful when I get to be a fantastic presenter.'
'I want to be a great presenter.'

All of these are in the future due to the words used; there is not the same feeling associated with these as saying:

'It is really great now that I have the confidence to speak in public.'
'I am really successful now that I am a fantastic presenter.'
'I am a great presenter.'

(continued)

And, of course, you want to 'jazz it up' a bit beyond that and you may have already read or heard people talk about affirmations structured along the lines of:

'I am so happy, grateful, and excited now that . . .'

. . . and then what follows is the thing that you are looking to achieve or change in your life.

Hence, we could tweak the previous examples as follows:

'I am so happy, grateful and excited now that I have the confidence to speak in public.'
'I am so happy, grateful, and excited now that I am really successful and a fantastic presenter.'
'I am so happy, grateful and excited now that I am a great presenter.'

Perhaps you are starting to notice, even if it's very subtle, that the way each of these types of statements makes you feel is slightly different.

The idea is that over time you tweak the words slightly here and there in your affirmations so that it feels even more real and exciting to you.

When you say those words, 'I am so happy, grateful and excited now that . . .' they put your imagination in the present tense and that's when you want to think about and daydream and imagine that confident presenter and speaker and know and feel, now, how good it's going to feel once you are really at that stage.

So, let's get on to the feelings now, and let me explain why this is so crucial.

Our minds are made up of two parts – you may already know this – the subconscious part of the mind and the conscious part of the mind.

The subconscious does essential things like pumping the blood around our bodies, breathing and lots of other important life things all on autopilot, so that we don't even have to consciously think about them.

The thing is – your fear responses are also on this autopilot.

You don't have to constantly think about things that you're scared of. If the situation arises, boom, you'll get scared, the subconscious has taken over.

So, if someone asks you about doing a talk, and it is something you fear, you won't sit for 10 or 20 seconds thinking consciously about whether or not you feel good about this request; more than likely you'll get that internal feeling of fear or dread come over you immediately.

Now, out of the millions of things your subconscious mind is tracking at any one moment in time, it's got to decide which are the five to nine things we need to be aware of in our conscious minds – because studies have told us that our conscious minds only track or pay attention to, on average, five to nine things at one time, which is your current awareness.

I call it the funnel of relevance, where the subconscious has got to take the millions of things in any moment it can pay attention to and get it down to just five to nine things to be aware of right now in this moment.

So, here's an example: how your feet feel in your shoes probably isn't in your awareness, but now I've mentioned it, it likely is. You see, unless you've got a new pair on today and they're absolutely killing you, how your feet felt in your shoes wasn't in your conscious awareness before I mentioned it.

If someone had drilled from below through the floor, you'd soon move your foot out of the way because the subconscious would have drawn your attention to that drilling or vibration and you would have moved your foot. But if you're engaged in something or you're reading this and you're fully engaged, you're probably not conscious until I make it relevant. How did I do that? By mentioning it, just talking about how your feet feel in your shoes.

Now, the same thing happens with lots of things in life. You may be at work, you may be at school, you may be at college, you're focused on something, your five to nine things are fully occupied . . . and all of a sudden somebody says to you, 'Isn't that fan noisy? Isn't that aircon unit noisy?' All of a sudden, you can't get that noise out of your head. You previously couldn't physically hear the noise that is now dominating your thoughts and now you can't get away from hearing it. That again is an example of something going from your subconscious into your conscious down that funnel of relevance.

With your affirmations, you need to feel you have already achieved them so they're in your conscious awareness, so that your mind will alert you to things that you wouldn't normally notice. Then you will have the ideas and inspiration to do what you need to do to make things happen for you.

Now, here's a good example of this. Many of you reading this will have experienced this in your life or heard it has happened to somebody else.

Let's say, you've got a car, a particular car, and you've decided you want a new car – a different car. You know the colour you want, you know the style you want, you know the precise model you want, but rarely do you see that car anywhere when you are out and about; until, that is, you get one.

Once you get that car, you see them everywhere, don't you? Now what do you think has happened there?

Do you think the universe has put a load more down there overnight?

No! They were always there, you weren't noticing them because your mind, the subconscious part of your mind – like most people's – doesn't think that things you want are relevant to you. It thinks that things you *have* are relevant to you, and that's what your mind pattern-matches on.

The only thing that's changed from when you were not seeing those cars to now seeing those cars everywhere, is you've gone from wanting one to having one.

Your emotional and neurological association with that car, if you like, is now one of having it; you've got it.

Can you see that overnight your subconscious has gone from showing you these cars hardly ever to showing you these cars everywhere you go?

There's not more of them out there. Like the noise of the fan that you weren't hearing, or the feet in the shoes that you weren't feeling, you were not seeing those cars.

Now my wife says the same thing happens with dresses. She wants a particular dress, thinks it's really rare; once she gets one, she goes out, three other women are wearing the same dress. It happens with everything in life.

Our mind shows us what it feels is relevant to us.

So we have to play a trick on the mind, if you like, and make it think we've got or have achieved those things that we really want to achieve and get to in the future. And when we do that, when we've got the right feeling associated and we feel it now – we've got that present moment feeling and how great it's going to feel – the thoughts, ideas and inspiration will come to us.

When we've got all that going on, that's when we start to notice things like the cars example; we notice opportunities and we have ideas, we get inspiration, we have different thoughts. And that's why the affirmations are so important in the present tense and why the feeling of having achieved it or having it now is key to making affirmations work.

Once you start to notice more opportunities and have ideas, then it's just down to you to take action when those ideas and opportunities come up.

You know, they say we have about 60000 thoughts a day – 90% plus of those thoughts are subconscious while on auto-pilot. So by saying these affirmations over and over again and getting used to them and feeling good about them – in the morning when you first get up, at night just before you go to sleep, and whenever you can during the day if you have a quiet moment or two – what will happen is it becomes like when you get the chorus of a song stuck in your head and you can't get it out. You will embed those sayings and the feelings associated with those sayings into your subconscious and they'll become an automatic part of the 60 000 or so thoughts you're having on a daily basis. Then what's going to happen is you're going to feel better, you're going to notice different things, because our minds notice only what we focus on and think about as relevant to us.

Visualisation

Visualisation is basically just taking each of your affirmations from earlier and thinking about them in a lot more detail.

It is where you rehearse and imagine future events in your mind. We do this all the time naturally, but unfortunately people all too often imagine bad outcomes rather than good outcomes.

If you are worrying about something, you are visualising it, you may not be consciously noticing every element of the visualisation – such as the pictures in your head, the inner voice or imagining or remembering something someone else or you said, or even sometimes the smells of the memory. One thing is for certain though; when visualising, people notice the feelings.

That's why sometimes when we feel bad about something, like an upcoming talk or anything in life, a good question to ask ourselves is 'What was I just thinking or imagining that is making me feel bad right now?'

Once you know what it is, you can either visualise it going better or you can use the affirmations or anchors that we have already covered – or of course you can go back to earlier parts of the book to deal with the thoughts and/or beliefs that are causing you to think in this way.

Visualising is so important as it sets your mind and body up for the real thing.

Sports people visualise before an event to practise in their minds and even in the moment before every shot or action. They have proved in countless scientific studies that our minds know no real difference between something imagined (visualised) or real. In fact, scientists have proven that when athletes imagine running a race in detail in their mind, the same muscles fire in the same order, even though the person is just sitting in a chair and not physically moving!

Someone with an extreme fear of spiders, for instance, usually only has to think of one or hear someone speak about them to get a fear feeling, because they have run a visualisation of something involving a spider and it has created the bad feeling.

One big thing to understand before we go any further, though, is that our subconscious minds cannot process negatives – we do that on a conscious thought level after the initial thought has been processed.

For example, if I say 'Don't think of a banana' – what happened? Even though I said don't think of it, you did!

This means that when people have affirmations or visualisations that focus on not wanting the negative – they've doomed themselves.

People often say to others going into a difficult situation 'Don't worry about it, you'll be fine' – well-meaning, but you had to focus on "worrying" in order to process what they said and that would have given you a degree of negative emotional response.

Far better to say to someone, or yourself, 'Stay calm and you'll be fine'.

This also happens in sport. I don't play golf but know a lot of people who do and they often confirm 'Every time I am about to take a shot and say to myself don't go in the bunker or lake, I do!' To process their self-talk they had to hear on a subconscious level – the level that really matters – 'go in the bunker' – and then the body actions often follow the mind despite our real conscious intentions.

I remember many years ago when my daughter was very young and learning to ride a bike. She had a habit of all of a sudden veering towards lamp posts and finding it quite impossible to avoid them. The reason was she kept thinking as soon as she saw one (i.e. visualising) 'I hope I don't hit the lamp post' so her focus was on the lamp post and her subconscious and neurology – including body movements – led her there.

This Is Why It Is so Important ALWAYS to Focus on What You Want, Not What You Don't Want

When a footballer goes through a bad period of not scoring, chances are their thoughts before a shot are more along the lines of 'Hope I don't miss', rather than 'Hope I score'. In the first version their mind has to imagine the ball not going into the net, whether they consciously notice it or not.

With the second version they have to imagine the ball going into the net. Same situation as my daughter learning to ride her bike.

Of course, this is exactly the same with public speaking and presentations. People who do not like doing them typically imagine it going badly, while saying things to themselves like 'I hope I am not too nervous' and many other counter-productive things.

Whether you realise it or not, you imagine and visualise everything before you do it. You have to, otherwise you don't know what to do. You have a thought, you might think about something as simple as turning on a light. What has happened very quickly in your mind is that you've seen yourself go over and push the switch. So, your body goes over and pushes the switch.

When you're in situations where there's a level of fear, you're visualising. These visualisations run very quickly – the pictures, the things you imagine in your mind, and the things you say to yourself – such that very often you don't even consciously notice them; but you're visualising something going badly if you're currently experiencing fear about a situation.

Whereas if you're imagining it going well, and at the same time that you're visualising it going well you're firing off your anchor from earlier, then you're going to feel a lot better and stand a much better chance of taking the action.

Think about a presentation you have coming up; or if you don't have one scheduled, just think about doing a presentation to a group of people.

First, go through your affirmations to get feeling really good about doing presentations. Remember: putting on some upbeat music that makes you feel confident, alive and that anything is possible is also a great way to change feelings quickly.

Imagine, like a daydream, going into a room and seeing the audience there; you are waiting to be introduced, then you are taking the stage very confidently, starting your presentation and seeing the audience enjoying it – and you are loving delivering your presentation.

You need to imagine in as much detail as you can, imagine what you might see, imagine what you might hear, even what you might smell. Visualise that in your mind like a scene from a movie, and fire off that anchor when you need it to for an extra boost of feel-good emotion.

I want you to play pretend like a child again with this and make those pictures in your head of you actually doing presentations and public speaking, which you once feared but now love, how you look, how you move, just see yourself doing it and feeling good about it.

If it helps, put on that music that puts you in a good mood; music is a great mood changer. When the music is underway and the good feelings are running, do your visualisation again, seeing yourself doing what you want to do and associating those good feelings with it.

If you do this a few times a day, every day for a few weeks, you'll recode your brain to associate different feelings with doing presentations; and every time you think about doing a talk, you'll automatically run this new visualisation and get the associated feelings – especially if you have dealt with most of the negative thoughts in earlier chapters.

Some people will get there straight away or after a couple of days, for others it may take a little longer.

You are basically developing a new habit – we understand that this takes 28–32 days; however, depending on the degree of fear you once had, and the positive emotions you can develop when doing the above visualisation, you can rapidly reduce the time – right down to minutes in some cases.

Everyone is different, and everyone reacts differently to things. Some people with an extreme fear may resolve it just by using visualisation and may not need to do any of the belief or negative thought exercises. Other people may make no progress until they have fully cleared the negatives. Still others will need to do a bit of both: some negative belief work to get their fear down a bit and then some visualisation, anchors and affirmations to get the fear down further and build their confidence up.

It is also important to point out that whether the biggest improvement comes from the negative thought work you've done or mainly from your visualisations, or some mix of the two for a given situation such as a talk coming up, this doesn't mean it will be the same for you in every situation in life – or even every presentation. It is all context based.

As an example, a talk to a room of clients may mean you need to focus on fear reduction and visualisation; you may find, however, that a talk to team members only needs you to focus on the visualisation aspects.

All these techniques, whether it is belief/fear issues or visualisation, only take a few minutes to do. They may be quick and easy to do – but they are also easy not to do!

> Affirmations and visualisations have to be done every day to develop that new automatic and habitual way of thinking about the area you are looking to improve in.

Hollywood Movies

Have you ever dreamed of being a Hollywood movie star, the main star in the leading role? Well, that is the secret to successful visualisation. You need to make these visualisations in your mind like playing out scenes from a Hollywood movie so that it feels that real and makes you feel that good. This is like going back to childhood when you would play pretend.

The great thing is that positive visualisation takes very little time, no one else knows you are doing it and it makes you feel good. Plus, of course, when done every day for a number of weeks it will start to change your life in the way you want it to.

The best way for me to explain how visualisations need to be from a detail perspective, is for me to share some of my own with you. You'll still need to develop your own, that have real meaning to you, but this shows exactly the level of detail and the emotional hook points you are looking for so that when you visualise it really feels good and makes you smile on the inside and usually on the outside too!

My bookstore visualisation

Some years ago, before I had even written a book – let alone got a publishing deal – I set myself the goal of becoming a published author with one of the world's leading publishers and seeing my books out in the shops.

Now thinking about it like that was in itself exciting for me, but it wasn't anything like as detailed or emotionally exciting as it needed to be to get real results. So here is the detailed visualisation I came up with for achieving this goal.

I would imagine myself walking down Charing Cross Road in London, and going into Foyles, the biggest bookshop in the world when I was much younger.

I go into Foyles and go up to the floor where they have the personal development books; they've moved Paul McKenna's books to one side to get mine in!

I go over to where my books are and notice that someone is looking at one of them. I go up to them and casually say, 'Did you know, the author is in the store today, you could get that signed'. They turn to me, they look at the back cover to the photo of me, turn back to me, there is a moment of realisation on their face, and I calmly say to them 'I'll sign it for you now if you like?'

Wow, that scene in my head would get me every time. How fantastic would that be! Yes, it's a bit ego driven, but whatever works to get the right feelings with the visualisation is what matters. After all, you don't have to tell anyone else what you are thinking. It's your secret.

Note – the small emotional hooks that made this real for me and feel even better were the things like the Paul McKenna bit – it made me laugh on the inside and feel good and that is what you want from visualisations.

This worked for me on so many levels, as I will explain. First, thinking about it in that way motivated me to feel like an author already – and I thought about this scenario so many times that when the opportunity to share my book idea with a publisher came up (Wiley, the publisher of this book and my other two books), I grabbed the opportunity and asked for the introduction. You see, had I not been visualising like this then when the opportunity came up I would probably have hesitated and missed the moment. Negative thoughts like 'They will think I am being pushy and they probably only want established authors' could have deterred me from putting myself forward. My exciting visualisation, though, made me take this opportunity when it came up.

Second, this visualisation helped with my motivation to keep writing the book when the going got tough. I knew I had to write at least 45 000 words and I am on about 5 000 words and I am bored. I don't want to write the book anymore and I am wondering if I can just give the advance back and walk away . . .

But then I thought 'Yes, the bookshop and "I will sign it for you now", brilliant' and back to the book I went, typing words as fast as I could with enthusiasm generated by my visualisation.

My own public speaking visualisation

My route to public speaking was an interesting one, as I explained in summary at the start of the book.

After I sold my business and achieved that success, I became fascinated with how people achieve success and realised that I thought about the things I was good at very differently to how I thought about the things I was bad at.

This got me interested in personal development and, for fun, I signed up to a couple of courses on personal development and how the mind works, as I was taking a long sabbatical from work at this point.

The second course I did said that they were holding a third course on becoming a licensed trainer in their personal development techniques.

Now, I had no intention of becoming a trainer, but I really wanted to be able to do public speaking – my biggest fear that I had shifted somewhat with my mindset work, but had not actually put into action as I wasn't working at the time and so had no real opportunities to give public speaking a go.

However, this third course meant that every day for the 10 days of the course I would have to stand up in front of people and do a short presentation. On the last day I would have to do it front of about 100 people. So, I signed up.

The course was about three or six months away, I can't quite remember now, but I knew I was starting to worry about it soon after signing up.

So, I created a visualisation.

Now, for the purpose of clarity, this was way before the bookstore visualisation described earlier and before I became an author. I've shared these visualisations here out of chronological order, simply because the bookstore one was actually much more powerful because my own visualisation skills had obviously improved over time since the ones I am about to share.

As I was starting to feel nervous and worried about the course, I decided to first build an anchor, as described earlier, to help generate good feelings. I didn't feel the worry was bad enough to deal with limiting beliefs and thought patterns, because I had already done that, this was just some uncertainty flying around as it was now becoming a reality.

With my anchor built and installed, as we say, I was ready to come up with my visualisation, so I thought: what would be a really great outcome? Again, being really big headed, I thought: well to be the best presenter on the course would be a great outcome and have someone tell me that at the end.

So that is what I used. I would see myself on stage on the final day, 100 people in the audience, doing my final presentation of the course, everyone laughing and enjoying it, then a huge round of applause from the audience at the end, and as I come off stage, one of the main trainers says to me 'Mark, that was brilliant, best presentation by far, well done'.

I just thought about that happening every day, a number of times a day, for the months running up to the course; sometimes listening to upbeat music and other times using the anchor as needed.

I felt great going on the course, though still with a degree of nerves, but I would never have got to that point without the visualisation.

You know what, on the final day the audience did laugh a lot, they clapped at the end, and as I came off stage one of the cameraman said to me 'Best so far'. OK, so it wasn't one of the trainers, and my slot was about two-thirds of the way through. But, it made me feel great and was a bit freaky given my visualisation. This person thought having seen about 60 of the 100 so far, mine was the best.

Changing beliefs, visualisations and other tools are all ways of making us take action when an opportunity comes up and puts us in a better head space to perform well. So we become the sports person that is on a scoring streak – always thinking about scoring; and not like the one on a scoring drought, now hoping they don't miss every time they take a shot.

Going on holiday

A lot of people seem to think that visualisation is a crazy thing to do, but we all do it all of the time. However, unless we design our own positive visualisations for what we want to happen, then – if it's something new to us – most of our minds will pick a negative visualisation. It's like an oversensitive defence mechanism taking over.

I'm sure a lot of people must do what I do when thinking about a holiday coming up, especially if it has been booked for a long time and you've been really busy and just can't wait.

When I'm in this situation, every day, and a number of times a day, I think about the holiday. I imagine I have shut down for the holiday, we are packing, driving to the airport, checking in, on the plane, landing, going to the hotel or villa, etc.

I'm also thinking about the fun we will have and the things we will do.

While I am doing all this, I am talking myself through it like a running commentary, and this running commentary is in a very upbeat and excited voice.

For me it is this upbeat quality to my inner voice – even when not saying it out loud (which I do when no one is around) – which is very powerful and excites me and encourages me to think in more detail and grow my visualisation even bigger.

You see, for me the tonality of my inner voice is key – it is this, more than clear vivid mental images, that excites me. We are all different when it comes to visualising – some people react better to the internal talk, others to images or other sense elements such as hearing or smell.

But I Can't Visualise, I Can't Imagine Great Scenes!

If you don't think you can visualise well because you can't 'see' clear crisp images in your mind, it doesn't matter – the feeling that you generate is the most important aspect. Whether that feeling is driven by what you are saying internally or the pictures you are making doesn't matter.

We are all different and different things work for different people in different situations. You may find for some parts of life the inner voice is the key driver of the feelings, or in other areas of life or situations it may be the images you create.

Another Inner Voice Strategy

I have just been talking about inner voices and the way we talk to ourselves in our heads. And yes, we all do it all the time; those of you reading this thinking 'Rubbish, I don't talk to myself in my head' – well, guess what, you are doing it now!

It is just that our inner voice has become so habitual that we run around on autopilot all day, without even noticing the many crazy things we are saying to ourselves that pull us back from taking action or getting involved in opportunities that come up in life.

Some years ago, I came across a great inner voice strategy for dealing with a negative voice you're struggling with using other methods of personal development and change.

I call it the 'Cartoon Character Method'. Actually, I don't. I actually call it the name of a world-famous duck that hangs out with a famous mouse.

How it works is very simple and it goes like this. Let's say you continue to think something like 'I have messed up so many times with presentations, I am never going to get good at this'.

You have tried various ways of getting rid of this, but it still haunts you and makes you feel bad every time you think about public speaking.

What you do with this method is – ideally when no one else is around, for reasons that will become apparent – you repeat the negative statement out loud a number of times, over and over BUT – when you do it you use the voice of a cartoon character that makes you smile or laugh.

So, for me, I would say that statement out loud over and over with that famous duck voice.

What happens is, like a catchy song chorus, eventually this becomes a habit that gets embedded internally and, whenever the original thought comes up, your mind immediately or soon after switches to the funny, squeaky cartoon version.

For many people, me included, this removes the negative emotion from the statement and in a weird way can often make me feel good about it. One of the reasons this works so well is that the meaning of anything said to us or anything we say to ourselves comes more from the tone used than the actual words said.

I have heard other people say that to get this to work they need to say the statement about 10 times per session and do three sessions a day for a week or more. For me, in most situations just saying it out loud 10 times, i.e. one session, means the emotion has changed for me to a level where it doesn't bother me. We are all different – and some issues have taken me a bit longer.

You can also use this technique if you keep replaying in your mind something negative or hurtful someone else said to you.

Remember when starting to work on reducing any fears or negative feelings to take that SUD reading – 0–10 – so you know, for example, before you start that, it's a level 7 out of 10 for you. Then, after doing a technique a number of times, you can ask yourself where you are now and measure your progress.

Over to You – It's Visualisation Time!

Now it is your turn. Take the time right now to sit down quietly and daydream about what doing that fantastic talk or presentation would be like for you.

You need to invest the time and build and practise this visualisation daily; the magic and change happens when you actually do this exercise and technique, not just read about it.

Too many people read a book to help them but do not do the exercises enough, or even at all, and wonder why they haven't made any progress.

Get a great visualisation going in your mind today – you can change it and enhance it as you go. Remember that one of the most important things is that it feels good and feels like you already are that great presenter or public speaker. It may well not feel like that at first, it may even feel silly or untrue, but stick with it, and use the anchor technique and/ or the music techniques to help generate the right emotions or feelings before visualisation, if that helps you.

5
Being Yourself and Dealing with Mistakes

One of the most important aspects of giving a presentation – in addition to getting the content right and making it interesting, which we are covering later in the book – is simply to be yourself.

One of the biggest mistakes that I've seen people make, when giving talks or presentations, is thinking they have to become someone else.

They think they've got to be this slick professional speaker that doesn't make any mistakes, where their presentation is highly polished and they deliver it like a performance in front of the Royal Family. Whereas, in all honesty, what you need to do is one thing and one thing only. And that is to be yourself.

This is the biggest transformational step that I took while getting better at public speaking. I started off buying all those books and reading all those articles – you know, the ones with something like 101 presentation techniques:

'Don't put your hands in your pockets.'
'Don't turn your back on the audience.'
'Don't do this . . .'
'You must do that . . .'
'If you don't do these five things the presentation won't be any good . . .'

and on and on . . .

It was all just too much for me. I couldn't remember 101 things. I couldn't remember three things to do when I got up to do a talk, especially in the early days when I was very nervous.

Then came the eureka moment when I just said to myself, 'You know what? I'm going to be myself'. And that is the biggest secret to my success in speaking.

My experience is that audiences love it when they feel presenters are being themselves. Audience members often come up and say, 'Mark, I love that you're the same person on stage as the person we speak to before you talk, and the person we speak to after the talk. It's refreshing, you're not lecturing to us, you're almost having a chat and a conversation with us'.

You see, here's the thing about presenting or talking about something. If something goes wrong in your life, say you are driving and your car breaks down and you have to call the rescue service. Then, they don't turn up, you have to call again, then eventually they come. They then inform you they sent the wrong truck and then you have to wait for the right truck to come. Then when finally they are towing you home, something else goes wrong and their recovery truck breaks down! And later, when you go and relay those events and all that happened to your family and friends, you become the world's best storyteller. You've just got to take that version of you, the brilliant storyteller talking about something that happened, to the front of the room. That's the person or the speaker right there. Not some image you may have in your mind of some slick professional speaker. People generally don't want the slick polished presenter. Pretty much outside of politics the slick presentations are not what people usually want. They want someone they can relate to, someone who's going to teach them something, share things with them, someone they connect with.

If you were to look on my website, you'd see that I've spoken for huge companies and I've spoken for small companies. I've even been trusted and asked to speak in Hong Kong to 800 four- to eleven-year-olds. Why? Because of the way I do my presentations. Because it's me and because it's just my friendly attitude of 'Hey guys, I've got some interesting things to share with you that I know are going to be of immense value to you'. Rather than coming from a very staid, polished presentation stance that can come across as a lecture.

Obviously there are some environments, audiences or topics where a very professional approach is needed, but these are few and far between. I have seen people bring their own personality and the real them to pretty much every type of presentation out there.

Mistakes

A lot of people worry about making mistakes. People think it's got to be perfect. But making mistakes isn't a problem – it's how we react or respond to them.

I'll often say the wrong word in a talk or I'll drop my flip chart pen. Many times I've even tripped over a flip chart leg.

When these things happen though, rather than get embarrassed and panic, I just make fun of it myself.

If I drop a flip chart pen I'll just say to the audience, 'I'm even throwing the pens around now. Good job I've taken out my public liability insurance'. Or if I fall over the flip chart leg I'll say, 'Oh, I knew I shouldn't have had those three beers before I started talking today'. With that response from me the audience always laugh and then they've very quickly forgotten that it ever happened – and so have I.

If you don't take a mistake seriously, and you make fun of it, the audience won't take it seriously either.

It isn't about not making mistakes, it's about not panicking and falling apart if you do make a mistake. The audience won't notice it; they won't care. In fact, you can make the mistake part of the presentation.

It's just about relaxing and being yourself. See yourself at the front of the room being quite animated, and friendly, and having a conversation with the audience and knowing in your head that you're going to deliver some information to these people that they're going to enjoy listening to, and that they're going to get value out of it too.

And how are you going to do all of that? You're going to do it with the next part of the book on giving a presentation and delivering great content.

PART TWO

Delivering a Great Talk or Presentation

6
The 'In-Motion' Start

So, the first thing that we need to explore is what I call the 'in-motion' start.

The secret to engaging the audience from the very start of any talk or presentation is to use an 'in-motion' attention-grabbing start.

The added benefit is that this will also help reduce any first-minute anxiety if you suffer from this – and I know many people do.

Now, what do I mean by an 'in-motion' start?

Well, first we need to talk about what happens before your presentation . . .

Before You Speak

Now, the first thing is that you really want to have it set up that somebody else introduces you, even if it's just a very brief introduction.

As the presenter, you don't really want to be the one that's having to get people to take their seats, be quiet and get ready, because you then risk having what I call a 'hesitation gap' and you don't have momentum at the start of your presentation.

The hesitation gap

All the time you are trying to get control of the audience, it creates a gap between you taking the stage and starting your presentation in which hesitation can occur.

In this gap you can easily start to feel more and more uncomfortable, or to feel like you've not got control of the room, and then start to doubt that people are paying attention or even want to listen to you.

It's then a slippery slope to panic and all those dreaded fears about presenting.

So, even if it's just a friend, get them to get the audience settled – it can be as short and simple as: 'Okay, can we take our seats now, please, because Mary is about to start?'

I'll cover more on getting people to introduce you later in the book when we look at preparing for the presentation day. But if that's not possible, then you can use what is called a pattern interrupt . . .

The pattern interrupt

If it's not possible for someone else to introduce you, then I find it's good to use what I call a pattern interrupt, which is to say something to the audience as soon as you take the stage that grabs their attention, for example: 'Okay, everyone. I've got good news and bad news' – then you have something funny to say beyond that, what the good news or bad news is.

People tend to stop when they hear 'good news and bad news', 'Oh, what is it? What is it? What are we going to be told? What's happened?'

But, as I said, the best thing is to get somebody else to introduce you, because then you can do this 'in-motion start' that I love doing that has really helped me to consistently engage audiences from the very start of my presentations.

The 'In-Motion' Start

If, while you are being introduced, you're standing off to the side or at the rear of the room, then you've obviously got to walk – whether it's five steps or 100+ steps – from where you are to where you're going to present from.

Basically, after you've been introduced, if you don't start talking until you get in position there's likely to be a silence, this gap that I call the hesitation gap. Usually, most people in the 'gap' – even if they are at the front of the room – are then fiddling with their notes, their laptop, etc., while the audience watches and waits in silence . . .

For instance, the person introducing you says: 'Here is Mary', or 'Here is Jack' – and then there will be this silence, or maybe the audience clap for a bit but then go silent until you get in position, during which time nobody is speaking at the front of the room.

You'll probably have to move into position, put your notes down, sort out your water and then go to start.

It's that gap between the audience being ready and you starting that is the hesitation gap.

So, what I always do, and what I get everybody that I coach and help with public speaking and presentations to do, is the 'in-motion' start.

As soon as they introduce you – as you're walking up – you want to start with the opening line of your presentation.

Now, if the audience do start clapping, then you need to just wait for that to die down slightly so that you can talk over any noise going on.

This simple technique doesn't leave a gap for the hesitation to occur.

It doesn't leave a gap for the audience to start thinking and wondering about you or your presentation, because you catch them off guard. You catch them unaware, because they're probably used to the gap; but you've been announced, you start walking and all of a sudden you're talking – and so they're listening and they're engaged.

Of course, the real power when they're engaged from the start is to begin with something really interesting. You start with either an interesting fact, an interesting story or a question for them to think about, something that captures their imagination.

What I use a lot when I speak is when the introducer says 'Now, we're going to hear from Mark Rhodes', and while there is clapping, I'll start walking up. As I get near the front of the room, at the point where the applause is starting to die down a bit so I know that I'll be heard, I'll just start talking and will often say:

'You know what I love about speaking? What I love about speaking is it used to be my biggest fear.'

Now, all of a sudden, I've got the audience, because they're thinking:

'Hey, he's up there speaking. He's doing a presentation. This used to be his biggest fear. What happened?'

Now, I know what you're probably thinking is: 'Well, that's all right for Mark. He does his talks about mindset. That story links really well with mindset. What am I going to do? It's easy for him.'

Well, you come up with something yourself. You think about your presentation, and you come up with something from your content that's really, really interesting. And you deliver that at the start, so that it captures their imagination and makes them listen and become engaged.

Here is a real-life example from a client. I was helping a lady who is an accountant, and she had a presentation to do to a room of GPs, i.e. doctors. When I looked at her presentation and her content, I found that her original opening was the typical sort of line that somebody does in the professions when they do a talk like this; something along the lines of:

'Hi, my name's Jane. I'm here today to talk to you from XYZ Accountants. We have got offices in town A, town B, and town C, and we've been established since 1827.'

. . . at which point most of the audience are just disengaged, because it's the same old boring information, and they're not really interested in how many offices Jane's firm's got or even where they're based at this stage or when they were formed. They might be interested in that as a bit of credibility later, if they know Jane can do something for them.

So, when I looked through the presentation – and I've obviously changed the names to protect the not-so innocent here – I found that way, way, way down somewhere at the end of the presentation, Jane was saying that they'd helped over 200 GP practices.

I thought: 'Wow, that sounds like a good number. That sounds like a very good number.'

I said: 'Jane, you need to start with that'. When you're introduced – as you walk up – you want to say:

> 'The reason I'm excited to be here is that over the last couple of years, we've helped over 200 GPs to run better practices, make more profit, and enable them to withdraw more drawings from the practice. And I'd like to share some of that with you today.'

Now, with an opening like that, a room of GPs are interested. They're paying attention. Here we have an opening statement that has got benefits that are relevant to the audience about what they're going to learn, and so the audience are interested.

It's a bit like the difference between me saying, 'I am going to do a webinar on public speaking', which still may get some interest, versus, 'I'm going to do a webinar on how to deliver presentations without fear that both you and your audience will love'.

It's a lot more interesting. It's a lot more compelling. It's a lot more engaging.

So, if I was doing a talk on public speaking, I wouldn't get up and say: 'Hi, I'm Mark Rhodes. I'm going to talk about public speaking.' Instead, on the way up, I'd be saying something like:

> 'So how many here would love to be doing presentations without fear, that you and your audience would love to hear?'

That's going to capture and engage the audience a lot more.

The key to this is for you to look for an opening story or an opening comment that's going to engage your audience.

If someone has introduced you by name, then you don't need to say it. If you haven't been introduced by someone else, I would still start with the same in-motion start and at the end of that, before going into my main content, I would then say something like: 'So. Hi everyone, I'm Mark Rhodes and let's dive in and see how we can achieve that amazing claim I just made.'

Engage them at the Start or Lose them Forever

The whole secret to getting the audience engaged and getting the audience's attention is to do it early on. You've got to do it at the very start.

It's harder to get people engaged if they have already disengaged. So you've got to get them at the beginning with the 'in-motion' start – a great opening, a great story, an interesting fact or situation or something like that; something that people are going to be curious about and want to listen to – and then the audience will think either that's very intriguing or that's very relevant to me.

Either of those, and the audience are going be engaged and listen to you.

Whereas, if you start with something boring, or you have a major hesitation gap, then what's going to happen is the audience are likely to disengage before you say your first word or most likely by the end of your first sentence. Worse still, they will start talking amongst themselves!

Once that happens you are going to have to do an awful lot to turn them around, because once they've gone it's very hard to pull them back.

So always have a great 'in-motion' start.

An Added Benefit . . .

An added benefit is that we feel less nervous when we are walking than when we are standing still. So, starting to present while in motion also helps to reduce any negative feelings; plus, knowing that what you are starting your presentation with is going to engage your listeners makes it so much easier for you every time. We are all excited when we have great news to share. That is what your opening should be like.

Even if you don't think you have anything fantastic to use, I bet you do; you just need to think a little deeper about something amazing, interesting or fascinating you could share with the audience at the start.

Here is another example. I was helping an energy company that do energy efficiency reports for very large building developments. I was helping them with a presentation and we were looking at what they would use for an opening.

Yet again – just like Jane from the earlier example – buried way down in their presentation was something about a project they'd been involved in or been called in to have a look at. This project involved a very big and famous upmarket hotel in London, we'll just call it the ABC Hotel for the purposes of this exercise.

They'd been called into the ABC Hotel and they'd noticed that the plans that they had for their development weren't going to be compliant with the new energy legislation when it was finished. They pointed this out to the hotel and, as a result, the ABC Hotel avoided wasting over £4,000,000. I told them, that's what you've got to open with. You've got to open your presentation with that story as soon as you're walking up, after they've introduced you and the clapping is starting to die down.

You've got to say something like:

> 'What we're going to share with you this evening is information that saved the ABC Hotel over £4,000,000. It stopped them making a major mistake in their development and I want to make sure that you don't make any of these mistakes with your clients, just because you're not fully aware of some of the intricacies of the latest energy legislation.'

You see, with an opening like that, all of a sudden that audience is most likely thinking, 'Hey, we need to listen to this. Not only do we need to listen to this because the topic sounds interesting, but also because it sounds like this person that's going to be speaking has got huge credibility. After all, they've just saved the ABC Hotel over £4,000,000. Maybe we need to pay attention here.'

I always learn and practise my starts like this many times before the presentation. If I need to sort my notes on the table once on stage, or position my stopwatch, I do all of that while I am talking. I don't stop once I have started. I never start with who I am or what I do, that just isn't as interesting as the 'in-motion' start. I usually get the person introducing me to say who I am and what I do and, if I do need to say it myself, I will say it after I have finished the 'in-motion' start and the audience are engaged with me.

7
Creating Great Content

Let's have a look at content then.

The thing with content, just like the in-motion start covered earlier, is that it's got to be interesting. The audience have got to find it interesting. And it's got to be delivered in the right order.

Regardless of anything else, no matter what topic you are delivering and what you want to get out of that talk, one of the biggest outcomes that you must focus on is delivering a presentation that people enjoy.

When making presentations, people often make the mistake of thinking things through in a chronological order. For example, if someone was going to be telling people about the development of something, they would typically start with the beginning and work through to the end in chronological order.

Now, as we know, with a lot of things it's the end that's the exciting and good bit. And all the steps along the way aren't as interesting as the big result or finish.

If you think you're going to reveal the big thing at the end of a presentation, like a pop concert where they sing the biggest hit at the end and everyone's waiting for it, that's not how presentations work best in my experience. People can often be disengaged before you get to the end.

You've got to start with your best content. And if you're going to talk about something that you're looking to get the audience excited about or engaged in, you've got to tell them at the start of the presentation what the great outcome or result is and then you can explain to them how to get there.

They've got to want the rest of the presentation when you start. So, you've got to tell them what it is they're going to get and how good that's going to be, and really build that up so that they want to listen to you and listen to the whole presentation when you deliver it. This is what the earlier examples of the 'in-motion start' were doing – starting with the great outcome first.

Stories Make It Much Easier

When you deliver talks or presentations, you must, as much as possible, use stories or worked examples.

Now, I never realised I was doing this in the early days. I'd done probably about half a dozen presentations at this point, maybe a few more. I was doing a presentation and one of the people in the audience who is a friend of mine came up to me (his name is Andrew – and that's his real name). He came up to me and said, 'What's great, Mark, is you use so many stories'. And I said, 'Well, I don't really use stories, Andrew'. He started to prove me wrong, referring back to the stories I had just told in my presentation. I replied, 'No Andrew, they were just worked examples'. It was at that point I realised they were basically stories as far as the audience are concerned.

When you explain something to people, you might tell them some facts, you might also explain the technical side of the topic and all the various ins and outs of it. However, you've then got to demonstrate these with a worked example or a story because then you make it interesting; that's how you make it real to them and how you make it easy to understand. If it makes sense, then telling the story first, or dipping in and out of the story as you share each stage or technical detail, is also a great approach.

I remember when I was once asked to speak for the Institute of Chartered Accountants in England and Wales at their Small Practitioners Conference.

I was going to be on after another speaker had finished their slot. This speaker, I could see on the agenda, was going to be talking about tax legislation. I'm thinking to myself, 'I'm going to be dead by the time he gets to the end of that presentation. I've got to sit through 45 minutes or an hour listening to some accountant go on about tax. Oh no, what am I going to do?'

Anyway, this presentation was fantastic, absolutely brilliant. I loved it. I didn't understand a lot of it, but I still loved it. Why was that? It was because everything was put into stories or worked examples. Either imaginary ones to demonstrate the facts or the concept he was explaining, or real ones from cases that he'd been involved in.

So instead of saying:

> 'Oh, if this happens or that happens according to law in inheritance tax under clause x and y, if you've been married and then divorced, then this would happen.'

What he actually said was along the lines of:

> 'Auntie Mabel has got three sons: John, Jack and James. James has been married three times and got four children.'

He'd tell this story like an episode of a TV soap opera. He had all these characters in the story that the audience could follow and understand the story and what was happening to them and their life situations due to the tax laws he was discussing.

I really enjoyed the presentation and learnt so much about tax law because of how he relayed the information: it was in a way that was meaningful and easy to understand.

For me, the big thing about great content is building it up into stories.

In my presentations, for instance, I would explain a concept at a high level – sometimes just say the name of the concept and then tell a story that was relevant to the audience and the presentation. Then, at the end of the story, I would link it back to the concept description I was talking about.

Most presentations I do flow like this:

In-motion interesting start
Funny or interesting story relevant to overall theme of event or presentation

First concept
Story that demonstrates first concept
Second concept
Story that demonstrates second concept
Third concept
Story that demonstrates third concept
. . .
Final concept
Story that demonstrates final concept
Recap/summary
Final thoughts
Ending impact statement or message.

I just move from concept to story using linking terms like:

'for instance'
'as an example'
'I remember one time'
'This always makes me think of . . .'

Of course, when I say a 'story', it might be a worked example, but it's something that gives the audience understanding, relevance and meaning.

When they get all those things, they like the presentation and the presenter.

Above anything else, stories keep the audience interested and they end up enjoying the presentation – which is of course one of the main outcomes you want.

Another big benefit of stories is they are easy to remember; you know the story and don't need a script or massively detailed slide. Also, when we tell stories we naturally use our tonality and reduce the risk of sounding boring and mono-tone. Most people would use great tonality with a line like 'and do you know what he then said to me . . .?'

The End is the Starting Point

When you put a presentation together, remember to start with the end in mind.

Ask yourself some simple but powerful questions about the presentation:

What is the outcome I want from this presentation?
What do I want the audience to be doing and/or thinking differently about?
What is it about this topic the audience need to know the most and what will help them the most?

Of course, if someone else has invited you to present, then there may be other people you need to ask the above questions of – the organiser, a typical attendee, someone in your company, etc.

There can be multiple outcomes, of course, and some will relate to the 'change' or learning the audience should receive, while others might relate to some action you'd like the audience to take – such as buying a product or service or finding out more about you or your company.

Think about this book. I didn't start out by explaining all the concepts and ideas I was going to teach you about doing presentations and public speaking. I didn't start out first by talking about myself.

The start of this book was Chapter 1 and the start point of any chapter is the title of the chapter. Chapter 1 of this book is called:

'How to deliver presentations without fear, that you and your audience will love, and you'll enjoy doing.'

You can probably see now how that title encapsulates the ideal position people want to be in with regard to public speaking and presentations. It covers the idea of the audience loving it, you loving it and you enjoying doing the presentation.

If this was a presentation and not a book, the Chapter 1 title would be my 'in-motion' start.

I gave you the end result upfront, so you were probably thinking: 'I'd like that end result and some of these other things Mark is going to cover, so I'm going to read this book and do what he suggests'.

I told you the big outcome at the beginning of this book, and then I started going into the steps to get there. And as I'm going through each of these steps, can you see that I'm doing in the book what I'm teaching you to do in presentations?

I'm even telling you stories when I describe a fact or technique. So, one of my techniques is to tell stories in presentations – and I've just told you a story about an accountant who delivered a presentation on tax, that was interesting because it involved stories.

I'm doing it myself as we're going through this book, using the same formula to keep you engaged and interested in the content.

Researching Content

This is about making a list of bullet points/topics/areas/ concepts that you need to share with the audience in order to get them to that end result you are promising in your opening 'in-motion' statement.

Basically, once you've got the big outcome/end result statement that you are going to open with and the other outcomes/ experiences desired for the audience, then you need to plan the rest of the content.

At the moment, we are just looking at researching chunks of content and ideas; in the next section I am going to cover how you structure it – just focus on content ideas and not how you could deliver it at this stage.

You may find you have all the knowledge and content ideas already, which is great and you'll be ready to skip on to the next section in this chapter. However, very often, unless someone is a recognised expert in the subject they are going to present on, they need additional ideas to help generate their content. That's where content research comes in.

There are many places to research content, but upfront I want to say that you must in most cases develop your own content and not copy anyone else's based on your research. Occasionally you may want to use something someone else has said and, if you do, I suggest you do what I do and give them credit in your actual presentation.

One of the topic areas that comes up in a lot of my own talks is confidence – and I said earlier in the book that I love a definition that Tony Robbins, the world famous motivational speaker, once gave. I always like to use this and say in my talks: 'We need to understand what confidence really is, now I don't believe in reinventing the wheel when something fantastic already exists, and Tony Robbins the world famous motivational speaker once said this about confidence . . .'

As I say, if you do use someone else's content, it should be a rare occurrence and be a very small percentage of your presentation – less than 1% I'd say – and you must give credit to the originator of the content. The 1% rule is my own guidance, and this doesn't apply if you are quoting technical facts or laws, etc. in the public domain.

This is how I think about content research:

When someone starts a conversation on a topic that you know a bit about, you respond with your own point of view, then they say something else and, out of what they say, you then have a further thought of what to reply. Now it's often the case that some of these further thoughts you've never had before or you'd never looked at the topic in that way before. It is the conversation and how the other person said what they said that caused you to think in a different way and come up with new perspectives or ideas about the topic.

So, with the research ideas below, these are suggested as ways to get the conversation started in your head to help you generate your own ideas or opinions based on what you come across other people saying in your research.

Here are some ideas of places to research online:

YouTube
Trade/industry websites
Blogs
Wikipedia
Internet search
Forums
LinkedIn groups.

Always remember to look at the age of any articles, as, depending on your topic, they may not be relevant today.

As I read or watch content, I am pausing and writing down my side of the conversation – my thoughts and ideas that have come out of what I have seen, heard or read, and I tend to put all of these into a text document or word processor on my computer or phone as I go.

It's a good idea to use a system, app or program for content ideas that can be used on your phone and computer and will sync between devices. This way, wherever you are when you get that brilliant idea, you can add it to your content store.

I think content is best built over time. Typically, I will have an initial slot of time to do some research and get some ideas down, then take a few days before my next content idea-generation session. In that gap of a few days I am thinking about the content from time to time or just having random ideas and thoughts to add to my list.

Content Order

Now you have some great content ideas, the next step – before getting into the overall presentation structure – is to get some sense of order and grouping.

I go through the content list I have gathered in the previous steps and group it into sections of related items that go together on some basis, like chapters of a book. I then use a spreadsheet or word processor and put down the 'Chapters' and under each I copy and paste in the content ideas to the relevant chapter.

Once that is done I go through each chapter and look at the most logical order to put the sections in. Using the cut and paste features, it is easy to move things around.

Once I feel that the order of chapters and ideas within each chapter is correct, I then go back through each chapter to see if I can create sub groups of the ideas within that chapter and create 'sections or segments'.

I then keep coming back to this, tweaking it and adding more thoughts or ideas over a few days – just a few minutes here and there. I allow my mind time to do its work and come up with new ideas or concepts to add into my presentation.

Once I am happy with the content at this level, I am ready to put it into the structure of my presentation.

Oh, and Just Ask!

Before we get into the presentation structure, which we have already started to look at of course in our content organisation phase, I want to talk about a simple and yet hugely powerful concept called 'Just Ask'.

I have had so many situations where clients have said to me they have a major problem with their presentation, either the content or delivering it on the day. Usually, they are convinced there is no answer and they need to just take a risk with their presentation; and they are then totally amazed when I reveal the 'Just Ask' concept.

Here are two very different examples to explain this.

I had been helping some senior managers in a bank prepare for a presentation to a client. This was a presentation within a meeting, so the audience was only going to be a couple of people, but that changes nothing, all the preparation steps are the same if you want to get the best outcome for you and your audience – be that one person or one million people.

We had been through content research, client research, etc. and met up a few days before the big day to review things. When I arrived, I was told that they had an impossible dilemma that could wreck the presentation and there was no answer – they just had to gamble. They even proudly told me I would not be able to help with it!

I suggested they humour me and tell me. They went on to explain that they didn't know whether just the manager and assistant manager should go to the meeting or whether they should take the four technical people too, 'making six of us and two of them' as they put it.

They went on to explain that if just the two go, there is a chance they may need technical help in the meeting and look stupid if they can't answer a question that comes up.

However, if all six go it might look like a coach trip and be overwhelming and even intimidating for the client.

Having explained it to me, they then proudly repeated their initial conclusion: 'So you see Mark we have a real dilemma and something you can't possibly help with'.

I then told them I could help with it, but they didn't look convinced.

It was then I rocked their world with this most simple solution:

'Why don't you just ask them? You could call them and explain you have two options for them for the meeting, in that some people like just the manager and assistant manager to come along and have the technical team on standby, and if needed we can phone them for anything technical, but other clients prefer us to bring the technical team of four people to the meeting, what would you prefer?' I said.

'That's amazing Mark, that is brilliant! Why didn't we think of that!'

People get caught up in the emotion and their concerns and forget that very often you just have to ask. This also means you go into the presentation not worrying that something isn't right or could go wrong.

The second example is very different again. I was actually doing something very unusual on this occasion and something I have only done a couple of times, because it doesn't usually come up as something people ask for my help with in the world of public speaking.

An ex-Director, now retired, of a large supermarket chain got in touch and asked for help with his huge public speaking fear for his father of the bride speech at his daughter's wedding.

Incidentally, this was another case where his fear level went way down once we had great content organised in a way that was easy to deliver.

That said, the main reason for mentioning this client is that on our second meeting, when we were going to finalise and tweak the content, he too told me he had hit a brick wall and had this impossible dilemma that I couldn't possibly help with.

He went on to tell me that other people had been giving him 'essential advice' and it all conflicted.

Some people said he had to tell embarrassing stories and make people laugh, that is what they expect from the father of the bride and the bride expects it too. Others said that the worst thing he could do was spoil his daughter's day by telling embarrassing stories about her. Just like the banking client, he too said something along the lines of there was no solution and he had to pick one option and just hope for the best.

Again I came to the rescue with 'Why don't you just ask your daughter what she wants?'

He looked confused.

I then explained that it wasn't going to be a surprise that he was doing a father of the bride speech, she knows that. So why not just say to her that this is her special day, and you want it to be perfect for her – and that some people were saying you should tell embarrassing stories and get the audience laughing, and others were telling you to avoid that at all costs – and then ask her what she wants?

He was blown away at the simplicity of this.

In summary then, if you are unsure about whether something will work or the best approach to take, just ask someone; not anyone, but the someone who matters most in connection with the talk or presentation.

Your Prompt Notes

For your notes on the day, ideally what you are looking to end up with is a list of bullet points or topic areas in the order that you will deliver them. This list has minimal detail about the content but just enough to remind you of the main things you need to talk about.

I call this list the 'prompt notes' and I call the bullet points in my prompt notes the 'tracks'.

I think of each bullet point as a song or track on a pop star's album. When they do a concert, based on the amount of time on stage and theme, they pick and choose tracks for that event.

I speak on many topics and over the years have built up at least 50 or more bullet points, each with stories/examples or 'song tracks' for each of my topics.

In an average 45-minute to one-hour speaking slot, I can only cover seven to ten bullet points or tracks, so I select the best ones for this event and sometimes mix and match between topics as well, based on what's needed. I'm never thinking about a whole one-hour talk, I am thinking about sharing seven to ten five-minute bullet points with stories or worked examples.

If you develop your content and presentations like this, it means that if, for example, you've got to do a 20-minute talk, then a two-hour talk or one-hour talk – and maybe the topics are a bit different – you just look back at all the prompt notes from previous talks you've done and all the different tracks or bullet points used in those talks. And you say: 'Well, I'm going to take four tracks from that talk, three tracks from this talk, and then put them in this particular order'. Then you've got very little, if any, new content development to do because you've done all of these tracks over and over again previously.

There is an example on the following pages of my prompt notes from one of my own Transformational Leadership talks.

The important thing is that I don't read from these notes. I glance through before I speak and write any additional thoughts on them; I have them with me at the front of the room and glance at them to remind me of the order and make sure I don't miss anything – they are a guide and a prompt, not a script. You could probably read them in five minutes, but they take me 60 minutes to deliver.

Leadership Prompts – 60 minutes

Love Speaking + My Sales v Speaking Strategies (In-Motion Start)

Skill Set; Mindset

So, What is this Mindset?

Thoughts Feelings Action Results – Recap my sales and public speaking thought pattern.

Shy and Confident Party

ATTITUDE AND APPROACH AFFECTS OUTCOME

Leader Mindset and Our Team Individual People Mindsets

People are ALWAYS doing the best they can with the skill set and mindset they currently have. Our job as colleagues and leaders is to help others develop their skill set and more often their mindset to achieve the best for all.

That woman's lazy! It's all about mindset!

What Makes A Great Leader And How Do We Develop Teams And The Next Level Of Talent?

Find Your First Follower

Leader Statement:

> 'To motivate the people they work with to achieve more than they would achieve on their own without our leadership'.

Give people something to belong to or be a part of . . .

UNHAPPY = REALITY v EXPECTATION

Many have to be BOTH Leader and Manager – BUSY PEOPLE USUALLY DROP LEADERSHIP PIECE.

Great Leaders Think Differently . . .

(continued)

ADAPT TO CHANGE AND FIND A WAY EVEN IF IT'S UNCOMFORTABLE – LEARNING TO DRIVE 1ST LESSON

Adapt to change – Attitude of 'How we can . . .' not 'Why we can't . . .'

FOR VISION/INNOVATION:

1. Ask better questions
2. What could I do better?
3. What could we do better?
4. What would others say we could do better? (CEO/MD Example coaching Managers) BARRY'S GOT A LIST NOW!

Being a visionary – what's likely to be the next big thing we can learn, develop, offer or get involved in?

Great leaders motivate and inspire people to be part of the common mission and goals and deal with rumours, blame and fear cultures as they are spotted.

THEY PAY ATTENTION TO:

Structure and Clarity – clear goals, a plan, well-defined roles within the group.

Psychological Safety – A culture where people don't fear putting their ideas forward or worry about being criticised.

Focus on Helping: 'How can I help?' – Staff come over.

Delegate well *and let the staff manage.*

IF YOU GET A CHANCE! – HEAD LIST

Genuine Recognition

At the end of the day our role as leaders is to:

1. Get trust with team members – do what you say
2. Inspire others
3. Help others
4. Set clear team goals *and make sure they happen*
5. Make sure people understand exactly what they need to do at a behaviour level to meet the Mission statement etc. and why . . .

Have an environment of 'Psychological Safety'.

Always be thinking 'How we could do this' and not 'Why it won't work'.

FINAL THOUGHTS

You tend to get what you expect and believe.

Negative world OR positive world of opportunities.

Inspiration is everywhere – even daytime TV.

Hawaii 5′O – Criticism – Say Nothing, Do Nothing, Be Nothing – Price was too high . . .

A Simple Presentation Structure

A simple process or structure is to start with that great outcome up front, and then cover each of the facts in some logical order and make sure that each one, or at least most of them, has a story or worked example to go with it. Alternatively, you could have one big overall project story or worked example that you tell, bit by bit, as you move through the presentation detailing each step.

If you're able to bring in a bit of humour here and there, it makes it so much better.

One section might be about you, your history, your experience. Another one might be different facts or points in the presentation. You think of all of those; each bullet point area that needs to be covered.

Now, I prefer not to have an 'about me and my experience' section in my talks, instead I prefer to have whoever is introducing me (if there isn't anyone, then ask a friend, business contact or colleague to do an intro for you) to read out my bio and experience. I then just mention relevant qualifications or experiences in passing as necessary during my talk, where it is relevant, and avoid that whole segment which can seem like you are reading your whole CV or resume out!

Next to each bullet point/track or topic you think about what story or example you could use to demonstrate that point.

Here is an example of a presentation I might do about Success Mindset:

1. In-Motion Start: 'What I love about speaking, is that it used to be my biggest fear'. (Tell story of how bad I once was and how I love speaking now and what caused the change.)
2. Skill Set and Mindset. (Tell story about two people making cold calls, one does it and one runs away scared – only difference is mindset, how they are thinking about it.)
3. Mindset Thinking Process. (Tell story about a shy person going to a party and a confident person and how they get a different result based on how they think about it beforehand.)
4. What is Confidence? (Explain Tony Robbins definition instead of a story.)
5. Reacting and Responding. (Tell story about my overreaction at parents evening for five-year-old.)
6. Expectation (Tell story about two school leavers, one expects to get a job and one doesn't and how it impacts their activity levels and performance in an interview.)
7. Fear of Failure (Tell unplanned outcomes story from Think and Grow Rich, plus my example about meeting five new clients but not winning any of them.)
8. Visions and Goals. (Tell my bookstore story and how the mind works with relevance when we want a new car.)
9. Final Recap of above and Final Thoughts
10. Closing/Call to Action/Big Finish.

This has seven 'bullet points' of main content, each of which has a story or worked example attached. There is the opening and recap and finally the closing. It varies based on topic, of course, but I work on the basis that each bullet point takes about five minutes on average.

The Big Finish

In the final part of the structure, I mention the 'Big Finish': you need to end your presentation on a high, leaving the audience feeling good, because you have said something either motivating or funny. And especially if you want that applause at the end, as they will do that if they feel good in the moment.

There are a number of things you can do:

1. Tell a funny story relating to the content or topic.
2. Tell a motivational story or just say a motivational quote that is relevant to the audience or occasion.
3. Even tell a joke people may have heard before but everyone will find amusing, and NO ONE WILL FIND OFFENSIVE.

Personally, while my talks always have humour in them, I don't think I have ever told a joke in a presentation or at the end. But, if all else fails and you've got nothing else, you can. You just need to position it by saying something like: 'I was going to finish at this point, but I was reminded this morning of a joke I heard some time ago and it made me smile again, so I thought to myself, I'm going to use that at the end of my talk, so here goes . . .'

And you have got to be certain the joke won't offend anyone.

I spoke at a conference where another speaker did this well. He had been speaking on social media and his joke was not connected to the subject at all, he just said he had decided to finish with a joke that the audience may have heard and that he really liked. It went something like this – Two people were in the jungle and came upon a tiger who was starting towards them. 'What do we do?' one said, 'Run' the other replied; the first one responded 'But we can't outrun a tiger' and the second one replied 'I don't have to, I just have to outrun you!'

The Power of Stories

As touched on earlier, there are a number of fantastic benefits to a presentation built on stories.

One is that you know the stories, so you're not going to forget your words. Most of the time, all you need is that bullet point in your notes or that bullet point on a slide that reminds you to tell the story. You see it and you may then tell a three- or four-minute story of that one little fact, but you know the story – you remember the story. You're not going to forget how it goes and you're not going to forget the words.

The other brilliant thing with telling a story is you will naturally use pauses and tonality in your voice, so you'll be an interesting presenter and will move away from the risk of being very monotone. Because if you're monotone, the audience will get bored very quickly. If you just read from detailed slides, again, the audience will get bored very quickly.

And the other thing is, if you've got a bullet point and then you tell a story that's not word for word displayed on the slide, you're no longer reading from slides like most presenters.

So that's the brilliant thing about telling stories. They make you a very interesting presenter because you've got the tonality, you've got the voice, you've got the pauses, you've got the interest, you've got the intrigue.

For me, great content is all about stories.

Start with the best content and start with the outcome – what they're going to get at the end, where this is going to end up and why this is of benefit to them. They want that, they want to know that.

Then you deliver the steps to them piece by piece with worked examples or stories that captivate them.

And that's content and that's how I do it.

(Remember too: develop each one as a section to make it easier to remember, easier to deliver using prompt notes and easier to re-use content in the future for similar presentations or talks.)

Humour

Usually, what I find with humour is that people like it best in my presentations when I'm making fun of myself – maybe something I've done or made a mess of in the past.

An audience is really drawn to you when you show vulnerability, when you show that you too can make mistakes.

That's why making a mistake in a presentation is not a problem, most of the time.

When people hear, for instance, that I smashed up my own car to get out of doing a talk once, that draws a lot of people to me. They like that. They probably think, actually, you know, I like this guy. He doesn't hide his failures. He doesn't try and pretend he's this great person who is better than us, and he doesn't pretend that he never fears anything.

With humour, you have to practise it. If you make the humour about yourself, people will find it funny every single time. People also like it when humour is related to everyday situations.

An important point when using humour: you've got to pause for a couple of seconds after delivering a bit of humour or a funny comment to give the audience time to process what you have said and then laugh. Too many people rush forwards with their next line of content and the moment is missed. I suffered with this once myself and I remember someone pointing it out to me after a presentation in the early days. He told me that I had some great and amusing anecdotes but I didn't give the audience time to laugh. One reason I did this was to avoid the deadly silence if no one did!

To overcome this 'what if no one laughs' issue, I developed a strategy for what I would do if that ever happened.

Let's say I have just made a comment which I believe is funny and the audience don't laugh, there is deadly silence; but I believe (may not be true of course) the audience suspect I was 'trying to be funny'.

In this situation I would simply pretend to make a note and say out loud, as I am doing it, so the audience can hear me: 'Note to self – never do joke about the duck in a suit, it doesn't work' – then the audience do laugh! At least that has been my experience on the few occasions I have had that deadly silence.

Slides and Flip Charts

Now, when it comes to slides I have a preference myself not to use them.

If I'm doing a talk of 90 minutes or less I will not usually use slides. I will use nothing if the audience is over about 80 or 100 people. I will just have my bullet point notes to the side and work from them.

But if the audience is around 80 people or less – it varies based on the room layout – I would ideally use a flip chart.

If you use a flip chart, you've got to make sure that everyone in the room can see it. Based on its positioning, how big you're going to be writing, how clear the pens are and of course the lighting and seating layout.

One advantage to using a flip chart versus using slides is that when you use a slide, the audience perception can be that you've put those slides together and just practised and rehearsed the material. So, it can seem like you're delivering a performance – led by the slides.

I believe an interesting thing happens when you use a flip chart. Not only do people often come up afterwards and say, 'I was so relieved you didn't use slides. I really like the fact you used a flip chart', a few other interesting things happen. One is that the audience are more engaged because there's more animation. You're moving, they're following the movement. They're not hypnotised and transfixed by this slide glowing out at them from the big screen. The other thing that I think happens is, because you're writing it up as you're talking, the audience have a greater trust and belief that you know your subject and are an expert.

Yes, you might be glancing at your bullet point notes to write the bullet point up on the flip chart. Then you tell the story, and while you're telling the story you might map out a little picture or scene on the flip chart. The thing is, because you're building it as you go, it's not pre-packaged like a set of slides – and the audience believes that you really know your subject, that you're an expert on that subject because you're standing there and building it before them. You're not coming in and saying, 'Look, here's one that I made earlier'. So that's why I love flip charts versus slides. Of course, it's just perception – because you could have just learnt and practised everything to just deliver with a flip chart – but I really think most audiences see it differently.

Practice in Segments

Now, if you've got say 10 bullet points in your 60-minute presentation, and you're practising it, it may be that there's only about three areas that you're struggling with and don't think are right. The great thing is that you don't have to keep practising the whole presentation – you can just practise those three difficult areas or segments over and over until you've got them perfect, and then have a practice run through of the whole presentation.

It makes it far more efficient to practise and rehearse because you'll always find that with certain presentations there are certain bullet points (tracks or songs) that you know really well and don't need to practise that much.

And then all you need to develop is what the hook or link is from one 'track' or segment to the next as you move through your presentation. Links from one bullet point or track to another can be as simple as saying 'another thing to consider is' and then you move onto the next point.

And that's content.

8
Dealing with Objections

What do I mean by 'dealing with objections'? Well, I mentioned this earlier when I was talking about how we get people to reduce their fear by creating great content that they know the audience is going to enjoy or love. You may remember the lady going to talk to a room of architects, where she went from a fear level of 8 down to 3 just through getting great content and dealing with the audience objections she thought she would face.

She was very, very scared. No confidence at all in her ability to deliver this presentation. And all we worked on was the content – making it more interesting and added the 'in-motion' walk up start.

I also said we dealt with some objections she thought might exist within the audience about her and her presentation, and then all of a sudden she was a 3 out of 10 and we didn't even have to use any actual fear-reduction techniques at all. A lot rested on the fact that her content wasn't there in a way that she thought would be interesting. Nor in a way that she thought she'd be able to remember it. She thought it was a boring presentation, so, therefore, the audience weren't going to enjoy it either. But a big thing for her too was that she felt that the audience would have objections to her presentation.

This female client was about 30 years old and was going to be presenting on a technical element of architecture. And she was going to be presenting to about 60–80 architects, they were going to be mainly male, and they were going to be around about 50 plus age-wise.

She thought – and it doesn't matter whether this is true or not because what she thought was affecting how she felt and her confidence – that they'd be sitting there thinking negatively about her presentation along the lines of:

'What does she know about architecture? She's not an architect and she's so young. What's she going to be able to teach us? What does she know?'

Therefore, she was worried that the audience wouldn't even engage with her presentation, they would dismiss it and her from the very start and not even give her a chance.

Now this is a problem that a lot of people have.

I've had people say things like:

'I have to talk to many male audiences and I'm female.'
'I have to talk to many females, I'm male.'
'I'm really young and the audience is much older.'
'I'm very old and the audience is much younger.'
'I think the audience will find the topic boring.'
'They will think they have heard all this before.'

And the answer to this is that you come up with an opening to your presentation that deals with the objections you think the audience may have about you as a presenter and/or the topic you are presenting.

Now the audience may not be thinking anything negative at all; but, even so, if you don't address this you risk ruining your performance because it is something that will be worrying you before and during your presentation.

It's the same in sales. If we think a potential client or customer is going to have an objection to our product or service, we raise it and solve it upfront so it doesn't get raised by them.

What I did in this case, with the young female architect, was tell her that what she needed to do was to open the presentation with something that addressed how she felt. So as soon as she was introduced, her walk up 'in-motion' start needed to be something along the lines of:

> 'Now, I know that all of you in this room have got far more experience than I've got in architecture, but I've been specialising in this very, very niche small area, and have got amazing results for other architects just like you. And what I want to do right now is share these ideas with you so you can see how this can be very helpful to you too, if you want to reduce costs and increase profits on your projects.'

Now you see, in that opening statement she has said to them:

> 'Yes, you're more experienced than me.'
> 'Yes, you've been in this longer than me.'
> 'Yes, you're probably think you are cleverer than me.'
> (Although they're probably not!)

She ticked all those boxes. And now they have heard that and it's out there, along with the reasons why they should still listen to her and the big benefits she can give them!

Even if they were thinking all of those negative things – and we don't know they were – they're now much more likely to think, 'Okay. Well, let's listen to this. Let's see'. They're going to start to listen and engage on a more neutral or even positive level to her presentation, rather than being negative about it and thinking things like: 'What does she even know? What can she teach us?'

So, instead of looking for the faults in her presentation, they'll more likely be looking for the value and benefits they can gain.

The big answer, in summary, is whenever you think the audience are going to have objections about your presentation or you, if you raise them upfront and deal with them early on they will probably change how they think and you'll be more confident when delivering your presentation as well.

There's another example I will always remember, and this is going back a few years now. There was an Independent Financial Adviser I was doing some coaching with on delivering great presentations that would help him to win more clients. This meant that when he was networking or when he was putting on his own seminars, he'd be able to win a lot more clients at the end of his presentations.

My goal was not only to get him more confident at giving presentations, but also to help him to develop a presentation that would lead to the audience wanting to take action and wanting to engage with him.

Due to the nature of the presentation, slides had to be used. This client wanted to use slides, I couldn't get him away from the slides and, to be fair, owing to his graphs and trends analysis a visual presentation was needed. Slides are fine as long as the whole presentation isn't on them. The slides are there to support the presenter, not take the place of the presenter. If the slides are just full of the text that the presenter is going to read out, then the presenter might just as well have stayed sitting down and let the audience read them themselves!

Generally, his slides were quite good. There wasn't too much information on them. There were charts that the audience needed to see. But we came to this one slide and it was total 'Death by PowerPoint'. It had so many bullet points on it, it was unbelievable. I didn't think it was possible to get so much text on a slide!

What's worse, he did not feel comfortable enough to split the content over more than one slide because when he was reading it he didn't even want to have to change slides! He wanted it all on one slide.

I said to him, 'Well, if you're going to keep that there, the audience are possibly going to think . . .when they see that slide, "Does this guy not know how to do slides or presentations? Doesn't he know that's not acceptable?" Or something like that'. I felt there would be some objection from the audience about this slide which was an unbelievable mass of text.

I thought carefully, then said to him:

> 'What we'll do, is we're going to put a little asterisk at the bottom of the slide before this one. When you've finished talking about the slide before the "Death by PowerPoint" slide and you see that asterisk, you're going to say to the audience: "Now, you've heard of death by PowerPoint I take it. Well, you haven't seen anything yet". Then flick to the slide and go: "Look at this baby".'

Now, because he's made fun of the slide himself, the audience are not so likely to take that slide seriously – they're going to see it as a little funny add on. We have turned a bad situation into a positive light-hearted moment in the presentation.

Sometimes people do end up with a particular slide where, for whatever reason, they feel they need to read from it. This can cause an amount of concern for the presenter because they worry the audience are going to be thinking 'They are just reading this off the slide, we could do that ourselves'. Again, the answer is to raise that potential objection yourself when you come to it, by something like:

> 'As it says on this slide . . .'

Or:

> 'I am going to read this next bit to make sure I don't miss anything out, as it's important . . .'

You could even add a bit of humour:

> 'So, like being back at school, it's story time, so once upon a time . . . .'

Raising objections upfront is a really, really important part of doing any presentation when you think there might be something about you, the topic or both that the audience might have a problem with or an objection to.

You simply raise it upfront; you put it out there and you raise it in a positive manner whenever possible.

9
Getting the Audience to Take Action

There are some other key skills that my clients often want help with when it comes to delivering presentations and public speaking. One is: 'How do we get the audience to take action from our talk? Whether it's to buy our product or service or to engage with me in conversation after? How do we make that happen?'

Now, don't stop reading if you think this chapter isn't relevant because you are not in sales! We are all in sales. More and more these days all roles have an element of selling, even in our personal lives. At the weekend you have ideas about what you'd like to do and your family members or friends have their own ideas. You prefer your ideas, so you are selling!

Getting People to Take Action after a Talk

One of the issues people have raised in the past is that they need help to motivate their audience to actually act. 'They say they will sign up for a workshop after a presentation but don't follow through' is something many people say.

Well, people will only follow through and do things if they really want the outcome being offered (so is it clear and compelling?) and there are consequences to them not taking that action there and then.

In some cases, people tell me that audience members have 'signed up', or said they will, for a workshop in principle, but they've not actually fully committed and paid for the workshop. They've signed up and said they'll do it, but then they don't get around to following through and paying and attending the workshop.

Generally, urgency and scarcity are two of the biggest motivators. And so motivating the audience to act through urgency and scarcity is one solution. They also need to understand the consequences, real or potential, of not doing it. Therefore, you really want to have those things in your talk along with the benefits they are going to gain and the losses they are going to avoid by attending this workshop.

You can create urgency through the date of an offer ending soon, whereas scarcity can be created by limiting the number of dates or spaces available. There are a number of ways to communicate both urgency and scarcity, but I stress that you must not invent them. They must be true. Do not ever get creative and suggest urgency and scarcity when it isn't true.

Remember Benefits and Helping

Sometimes, when someone presents and the end game is looking to win customers or clients, they feel awkward because they feel they are selling if they start to talk more about what they do or the products and services they have available.

The first mindset switch, therefore, is to forget selling and focus on helping.

Given what you do, who can you help the most and how can you help them?

The big thing to remember is that in most situations people buy for benefits – i.e. what the product or service will do for them – and not based on features or services.

Because where you want to be coming from with selling, in reality, is a position of helping people: you've got benefits to your products or services and you're looking for the people that need your help. No matter what you do, whenever people buy your product or service – it doesn't matter what it is – they are buying it to achieve something or to help with something or to do something. So, at the end of the day, everything is about helping.

There are benefits to everything that we offer as products and services. We just need to dive in and find them and package and present them in a way that the audience that we can help – the consumer, the customer, the businessperson – is aware of those benefits that are relevant to them, and we match them together.

Constantly, even when I am mentoring clients, I'll work with them, I'll drill them, month in, month out: benefits, benefits, benefits. They send me an email to review that they're thinking of sending out to a potential client and it's service,

service, service, and no benefits. You've got to get into the mindset of talking about benefits all of the time. So we're going to look at that right now.

Benefits are all about what they are left with after they've consumed your product or service.

What happens to them next? Is their life easier? Are they making more money? Are they healthier? Are they enjoying time with their children? Are they not worrying about things anymore? What are people left with after they've used your product or service? Because that is what you've got to sell.

You've got to sell the benefits they are left with afterwards. Which is why, using myself as an example again, I sell what I do on the benefits of winning more sales, having more confidence and those sorts of things, rather than mentoring or workshops or presentations or talks.

What are they left with after they have consumed or used your product or service? Think about that.

To get to the benefits, what we actually do is quite simple: we list our products or services and next to each one we say, 'Which means that', and then fill in the blank. So, if I use Sales Coaching or Mentoring as the 'product or service', I'd say:

> Sales Coaching/Mentoring *which means that* you win more clients.

Another example might be:

> Public Speaking Training *which means that* you could have more confidence to speak in public and overcome your fears.

See how it works?

Or another way to do it is you can play a game with yourself called, 'So What'. So, I'd say:

'I do coaching and mentoring.'

So what?

'Well that means that people get better at talking to potential clients or customers and can get better in sales presentations.'

So what?

'Well, that means they sign more deals.'

So what?

'Well that means they win more sales.'

So what?

'Well that means they make more money.'

Ah, now, you've got a really good benefit here for most people: make more money.

You Need a Compelling 'Why You' or 'Why Us'

You need a compelling 'why you' or 'why us' so that when somebody is engaged in looking at your website or they are looking at the literature you've sent out in your information pack, you're talking to them at networking or you are in a pre-sales meeting or you are in a sales meeting, you can say why they should deal with you. That's what they need to know. Why should people use you and your business?

You can use the benefits from before: your experience, your track record etc. Very often if people ask me what I do, I first go with a benefit statement. Then they usually say, 'Oh, how do you do that?' and then I'll say, 'I'm an author, speaker and mentor'. And they may then say, 'Oh, we have used business coaches before' or 'there's a lot of business coaches about'.

What I need to do at this point is differentiate myself from the masses. And I do that with my compelling 'why me'.

So, in this example, I'll say: 'Well you see, with myself, I've been there and done it in business. It's not just theory. I have owned my own business, I've started it from scratch, I built it up, and I successfully sold it. I've got proven results, proven testimonials. I'm also a published author. I've also been fortunate to have been featured in press, articles and career magazines due to the results I help people get'.

All of a sudden, it seems that there is quite some difference between myself and many other people in the market they might have come across before.

Now, I know that you may not have all of those things in your own compelling 'why me' or 'why us'. But you will have other things: things you have achieved, things you have done and things that make you different. Let me give an example that's not about me.

I was working with a client and she was involved in getting planning permission for large-scale developments. And what had happened is she had put together a proposal for a project and asked me to review it as part of the mentoring we were doing. And of course, what I like to see straight away in a proposal is something that says to me: 'Wow. These are the people that we need to work with'. So prospective clients are already thinking, 'Wow, these are the people that we want to work with' before they have seen your price and before they've read anything else.

And as is usual with clients in the early stages, this proposal didn't do that. And so I said, 'We need a compelling "Why us" at the front, a compelling "why you". Tell me something about some great results you've had. When have you got a great result for a client, but you didn't think you would? When have you exceeded expectations?'

And she thought about it and she said, 'Well you know what, a couple of months ago, we got a project approved for planning permission that nobody thought was ever going to get through'. And I said, 'Well, tell me about it'. She said, 'Well, there was this project, it was in sight of a very famous landmark, within three areas of outstanding natural beauty and yet we still got it approved!' I said, 'Wow, that's what we need to be starting with. Right at the beginning of this proposal, we need to be telling people that what you do is help people get their planning permission approved – and you can do that where most others can't. For example: "We recently got a project approved, within sight of a world-famous landmark, within three areas of outstanding natural beauty, that nobody else thought would get approved. But we achieved that."'

You see, coming up with things that can go in your compelling 'why you' or 'why us' – it may be big companies you have worked for, things you have done for people before – really has an impact on their first impressions.

So, you need to think about what these are for you. Again, they don't need to be hugely dramatic or world famous – they just need to be compelling and relevant to the person you are looking to win over.

How Will You Talk about What You Do?

Now, I want to talk about your opening statement. What you say when people ask 'What do you do?', because you'll want to refer to this in your talk or presentation at some point.

Obviously, you want this to be benefit based, and so there's this very simple formula that has three components to it:

1. The first part of this is that you say, 'I/we help/show/train', whatever it is – whatever that word is that goes in there about what you do – and then you name your target market. Followed by
2. 'to do or have', and then you give one or two benefits of your product or service and then
3. the ultimate emotional gain.

I'm going to give you an example right now that will explain all of this to you and exactly how this works.

So, if I were talking about myself helping people in the legal profession to win more work, then I would say:

'I help lawyers' (target market)
'to win more clients or make more fees' (the benefit)

and then I need to add in an ultimate emotional gain. Which would be, perhaps:

> 'to stop worrying or wondering where the next client or future fee income is coming from' (ultimate emotional gain).

So, as an example, here it is: 'I help lawyers to win more clients and generate more fees, so they can stop worrying or wondering where the next client or future fee income is coming from'.

So, as you can see, we've got the 'I help', because in my case it's about help. We also have 'lawyers', target market, benefits of 'win more clients and generate more fees'. That's the benefit in there. And then it all means that 'they can stop worrying or wondering where the next client or future fee income is coming from'. That's the ultimate emotional gain.

In one of my earlier examples, we looked at helping and I suggested you do an exercise to look at the benefits of your products and/or services and write them down. So you've got the benefits of your services already if you did that exercise. To get to the final piece of the statement – the ultimate emotional gain – you need to think about what happens when you finish, when you have solved that problem for people and they've got that benefit or service – what is life like for them now, how has life changed for them?

> What were they worrying about, but don't anymore?
> What frustrations did they have, that we have removed?
> What are they going to be able to do more of?

So, let's say, for example, someone had a skin cream product that was designed to help with rashes that itch badly and don't look very pleasant. Then they could say:

> 'I help people with skin conditions that itch to stop the itching, so they can get on and enjoy their life without feeling self-conscious when out in public.'

Can you see how this works?

Just three elements:

1. I help/show/train etc. (target market)
2. to have (the benefit, one or more of the benefits of your service)
3. so that they can (ultimate emotional gain, how their life changes as a result of that benefit or service).

You can have as many of these statements as you want. You see, the thing is you can build lots of opening statements and you just change the components according to where you are. In that previous example I was talking about lawyers, if I were going to an accountancy conference, I'd say accountants.

Now in that case, my benefit statement and my follow up ultimate emotional gain will stay the same. But sometimes where there are different markets for different products, the ultimate emotional gain would change too. It might also change based on what you know the audience or person you are talking to is currently going through.

So why not list a number of different examples of opening statements to say in various circumstances based on the different type of people you can help that you are likely to meet or present to?

Remember: you needn't be in sales to do this. You could be in HR and come up with something that explains to co-workers, staff and people you meet at networking or events what you do. You'll sound more interesting and be more remembered than the person who says 'I'm in HR'.

You adapt opening statements and change them to be relevant to the situation that you find yourself in. And you'll find that with a great opening statement, when you say what you do at a networking event or to somebody you meet in business, all of a sudden it's not, 'Right, okay'. It's, 'Right, okay, that sounds really interesting. Tell me more'.

When to Speak If You Have a Choice

One of the first things I always say to people is: if you're speaking at an event where there are going to be other speakers, then you want to speak early on in that event.

Ideally, you want to be the first speaker or the second speaker of the day.

If it's a whole day event, you want to speak before the morning break. You do not want to speak last or at the end of the day. That's my opinion.

A lot of speakers see the last speaker as being the "main and best" of the event. But I would still prefer to speak earlier in the day. The reason is, if your intention is to engage with the audience after the talk and you want them to take some action – to get in a transaction with you or something like that – if you speak early in the day, you're around for the rest of the day. Then, at every break and at lunchtime, the audience know who you are because you've already spoken and they can come up to you and talk with you.

If you're not speaking until much later in the day, there's a chance most of the audience won't know who you are during breaks and won't even speak to you in the breaks before your presentation. But if you've spoken already, everyone is likely to know who you are and some are going to come up to you. They're going to talk about the presentation and tell you they enjoyed it, and ask you some questions. And you're then going to have that opportunity to engage with people.

If you're the last speaker or you speak after the final break in that last segment, then people are going to be thinking about getting the train, getting in their car and out of the car park, getting on the road before it gets busy, and they're not going to hang around to talk with you after the event ends.

Nothing like if you speak earlier in the day.

Speak as early on in the event as you can is my advice. If it's just you speaking, so it's your event, then have something after the talk that people are going to stay around for so there is that chance to network.

Relevant Content

Aside from the time of your speaking slot, the biggest thing you need to do to get the audience to take action from the talk is to have content that is very relevant to the audience.

Have the content cover the typical problems the audience may have that you can help with and explain the results that people can get from your product or service if you're looking for them to take action.

Seeding

Make sure that the presentation is what I call 'seeded'. This is where you use examples that are relevant to the audience. You perhaps ask them questions that you're not even looking for them to answer out loud but to answer in their heads.

For instance, you might say that a number of times you've helped people in a certain situation to overcome it and get to a new stage, and then you might seed it by saying:

> 'And I'm sure a number of you in the audience here today can relate to this. In fact, there's probably some of you in the audience right now that are in this very situation or know you're going to be in this situation soon.'

So that's seeding, that's getting the audience to go, 'Actually that's me. Yes, I am in that situation' or 'Yes, I do need that'.

Selling at the End with a Call to Action

People will sometimes say to me: 'I'm okay doing presentations. I like doing presentations. But I want to be able to sell or get people to buy, so I need to have a call to action that gets people to buy, how do I do that?'

Well, the thing is with a call to action, if you've already got your presentation tailored so you have got the right message, to the right people, who have the right need, at the right time, they will usually take action. If you've got the right people in the room and they're not taking action, then they either haven't got the need or your message isn't convincing them that what you've got to offer will satisfy their need.

A sale happens when a customer's need and your message coincide in time. So, when a customer or a client has got a need and your message that solves that need coincides in time, then the sale happens – or at very least stands a lot more chance of happening.

So, if you want people to take action, they've got to really believe – through the benefits that you've spoken about, and through the case studies and testimonials you've used to back that up – that you can help them and that what you're going to do for them will probably work. And ideally, if it doesn't work, that they'll be still be okay, which you can achieve through refund opportunities or other guarantees to put things right.

If we list all of the reasons why people don't take action or why people don't buy something, they're usually risk related:

What if it doesn't work for me?
What if it's a waste of time?
What if I can't do it?

Risk is such a big barrier that if you're able to build in a guarantee it can help increase sales greatly as you have reduced or even removed the risk.

With all my speaking engagements, I say to people during the sales process: 'If you're not satisfied, tell me within

24 hours and I will refund you'. No one has ever claimed on that. No one. Because if I don't think I can do something, I say to people, 'Look, let's not go any further, I can't do that. I can't help you with that. I'm not best placed to help you with that'. But if you can remove or minimise the risk that the other person perceives, then it's going to be much more likely they're going to take action and buy.

In summary, you've got to explain your benefits, the customer has to have the need and your message needs to coincide in time with their need. Highlighting urgency and/or scarcity, if it's genuine, also motivates people. Equally, removing the risk they see also increases the chances of someone committing to what you are offering. And let's not forget the powerful ultimate emotional gain they could be experiencing or living soon.

Remember that urgency can be created with a time deadline; for example, if you book or buy in the next three days you can get the discounted price. Scarcity can be created when you are low in stock or have only a few dates available so people know their chance may go if they don't act quickly.

Other Elements

Near the end of your presentation you could also say something along the lines of:

> 'If you've got any questions or I've mentioned anything today where you think you might want some help, just feel free to talk to me at the breaks.'

Just put something like that in your presentation and let them know. Because a lot of the time, people don't think they can just come up and talk to you or believe you've not got the time. You've got to invite them and let them know you're open to them coming and talking to you after your presentation and throughout the day.

10
Dealing with Audience Questions including Difficult Questions

Time and time again, people tell me one of their biggest fears of public speaking or doing presentations is being asked a question they cannot answer.

What do we do about difficult questions?

Now, there's a few things on this. The first thing is – and this helps with timekeeping – in most presentations we don't want the audience shouting out random questions. It's usually better to say to people:

> 'I'm happy to take questions at the end, unless anything is stopping you learning or understanding, so what we're going to do is hold all questions to the end of the presentation and have a Q and A session then.'

And that takes the pressure off getting questions during the presentation.

Ideally, you want to finish your presentation, get the applause, step aside from the main speaking space and then have the organiser or host say something like: 'So, has anyone got any questions for Mark?'

If someone still asks a question part way through your presentation, then just say, 'I'll deal with that at the end if I may in the Q&A segment'. Unless it's obviously something very simple where they've just misunderstood a point. Just let the audience know early on in your presentation how the Q&A side of things is going to work. Whether they can ask questions throughout the presentation or if there's going to be a Q&A section at the end. The audience then know how you want this to work. You are the presenter and it's your choice.

Then we come to the issue of: 'What do we do if they ask us a question we don't know the answer to?'

When people ask me about this, I ask them how many times it has happened; often the answer is 'Never' but sometimes it's 'Well, it's happened a couple of times'. And I've then asked them, 'Well, why was the question difficult?' It's turned out that the question was so unique and specific to the person asking it that it wasn't relevant to most of the people in the room!

So generally, if we get a very difficult question, if we know it's very niche or specific to a limited number of people in the audience, we could say:

> 'Well, actually that's a very niche specific question. What I'll do is I'll pick that up with you at the end. So, meet with me at the end and I'll pick that up with you. And

anyone else who wants to know, and is interested in this, just join us at the back of the room at the end of the day and I'll run through that with you.'

This also gives you time to think about it and think about what the answer might be – or do a quick Google search on your phone at a break!

If you get a difficult question in the normal Q&A section, and you think that it isn't very specific or niche and it's maybe something you should know the answer to, don't panic! It could be that the way they're asking the question means you are not connecting it with your knowledge and don't really understand what they are asking. One of the things I do in this situation – if somebody asks me a question and I think, 'Oh, I don't know. I don't know' – is I buy time. I say to them:

'So, can you give me an example? Can you give me a specific situation when that has happened?'

or

'When did that last happen?'

or

'When have you experienced that?'

This does two things. First, it buys me time, as while they're giving an example, I've got time to think about what the answer might be. Second, what's probably going to happen is that while they're giving me the worked example or the story, or the 'for instance' around it, I'm going to realise what it is they're talking about and I'm probably then going to have an answer. Or worst case, you turn can around and say, 'Actually, you've caught me a bit off guard there, great question. Can we talk about that at the end?'

Then just move on.

You're the presenter, you're in control of the room.

How to Actually Answer Questions

When someone asks you a question, make sure you are looking at them while they ask it. However, as soon as you start to answer the question, make sure you are looking at the entire audience and sharing the answer with them.

Now, a couple of things: if you feel the whole audience may not have heard the question then repeat it to the audience before you answer it. It can be a good idea to include the question at the start of the answer to underline the fact you are directly answering the question, as people often deflect or side step them. For example, someone asks 'What's the best way to deal with difficult questions?' – I would typically respond with 'The best way to deal with difficult questions is to . . .'.

When I said earlier to look at the person who asks the question and then look at the entire audience when you answer it, there are a couple of reasons for this:

1. If when answering you just look at the person who asked the question, the rest of the audience can feel excluded and naturally disconnect or start

conversations with people around them. It can feel to the audience that you are now having a private one-to-one conversation with one audience member. Everyone has the opportunity to learn from other people's questions and your answers. So present the answer to the whole room.

2. If you just look at the person who asked the question and not the entire audience, it can also seem to the individual that you are now in a private one-to-one conversation and they will more likely feel compelled to ask you a follow-on question and keep the 'private conversation' going. If you are answering to the whole room though, and out of the eye contact range of the original question asker, then they have to actually interrupt you again and get your attention to carry the 'conversation' on.

This can also be a useful technique to use with what I am going to cover next.

People Who Keep Asking Questions

Occasionally we come across a person who keeps asking questions, either throughout the presentation or in a sequence, one after the other; every answer you give, they come up with another question.

This is an interesting thing that can happen from time to time and I find it almost an adventure to try and figure out why they are doing this.

Some possible reasons are:

1. They genuinely don't understand and need help.
2. They are trying to prove the presenter wrong.
3. They are showing off to the audience how much they know.

I can often spot number 3 by the start of their question, which will start with 'Isn't it the case that . . .' or something similar.

The way to avoid the obsessive question asker is to say that questions will be at the end. And if a question does come up you can say you will pick up on that at the end or in private with them.

If you do answer a question in the presentation from one of these people (or anyone else), remember to break eye contact with them once the question is asked and give the answer to the whole audience.

The scenario rarely happens in my experience, but if it does and all else fails, simply apologise and say that given the amount of content you need to get through and time available, while you'd love to answer all these questions, could they please catch up with you at the end and you'll spend as much time with them as they need to get their questions answered.

Incidentally, usually these people don't find you at the end; after all why would they? They no longer have an audience to perform to!

Getting Paid for Speaking

I needed to put this next section in the book because so many people ask me about this; but I wasn't sure where to put it! Why not put it at the end of the chapter on difficult questions seemed to be the answer!

A 'difficult' question I often get asked about speaking and doing presentations is: 'I actually want to get paid for speaking. But I've not really done it before, what should I charge?'

When I started speaking, I started speaking for free to get feedback and to be out there in front of people. I started going to networking events, and networking organisations, and speaking for free. Thinking back I was a little bit fortunate that a few of the first talks I did were actually paid, because they were for companies I'd already done some consulting work for with my IT skills, and I just charged them the same rate as my IT Consulting in previous years.

I then went through a period of not getting paid which is when I did free talks.

Then I started to run my own events. I joined a networking group. I would charge just a small fee: £10 for members of the networking group to come and attend a talk and workshop and learn from me. It was also a great opportunity to start collecting testimonials from the audience that I could use on my website.

I started like that. Then, after a time, I got to the stage where companies would start to see me speak and say, 'Hey Mark, how much to come in and talk for us?'

That's where you have to start working out what you will charge.

It is a bit of a minefield to start with. However, by getting in there, starting at a lower price, and gradually increasing your price as you go, it tends to find its own level as to what the rate is for you.

You tend to find that every talk you do the fees increase a bit. I guess if you're starting out, I would ask people who query fees if have they used speakers before, and if so who have they used. If you've heard of who they've used before, you may have a good idea of what sort of money these people are used to paying for speakers. And then you know where to position your value and the fee.

11
How to Prepare

This chapter covers a number of things you need to do on the day – such as slide, flip chart and mic tests – but they are included here, rather than in the next chapter (Delivering on the day), because you need to discuss these with the venue or organiser in advance, so you both know who is supplying what and what is available to you.

Your Bio

For some talks you will need a bio which tells the audience about you and your presentation. These are usually used for two main purposes.

1. First, for marketing materials, in the audience invite, on the event website and for any agendas or booklets given out on the day. Often there is a word limit for these, so you need to understand this way in advance and what date they need your bio by.

2. The second reason a bio is used is for the person hosting the event to introduce you. This can sometimes be the exact same document as used for the marketing materials, but it will always need one slight

tweak – a few words added to the bottom that I will cover in the next section. Often, though, you need to prepare a shorter version of the bio for the introducer to read out.

Opening applause and your introduction

A presentation starts well if the audience applaud when you are introduced. There are many factors that influence whether an audience will applaud as you go to the front of the room and the biggest factor is down to the person who introduces you.

An audience doesn't always know whether they are supposed to applaud or not in some situations, so they have to be given permission – unless you are lucky and a few do start it off and then others follow. The best way to achieve this is to add to the bottom of the bio version being used by the person introducing you 'Now please give a warm welcome to Mark Rhodes'.

Incidentally, even if you have sent this in to them in advance, take an extra copy on the day in case they haven't got it with them.

What should the bio include?

The bio should start with what you are going to give the audience, what they are going to learn or find out about, and it needs to be positioned as a benefit to them. In my opinion, this must come before anything about you or your background.

Even if you are not in sales, it seems the earlier chapters related to selling could be useful for writing this bio as you are now selling yourself to the audience. A simple framework might be:

1. The outcome/big benefit of this presentation
2. Why this speaker
3. Major project/clients/achievements relevant to the topic or event
4. Advice about audience questions
5. 'So please give a warm welcome to . . .'

For example, let's say I have been asked to do a talk on Sales and Winning More Business:

1. Our (next) speaker, Mark Rhodes, is going to show you how you can easily win more sales and business without putting in lots of effort and, what's more, if you have to sell as part of your role – but would never call yourself a sales person – Mark is going to help you with that and make it so much easier.
2. Mark Rhodes has been there and done it himself in business, made major sales in SME type situations and huge corporates and helps people every day to win more business through his talks, trainings, and books.
3. Mark has been a keynote speaker at the Institute of Sales and Marketing Managements main annual National Sales Conference, is a published author and has been featured in press and media.

4. Mark will be answering any questions you have at the end of the presentation so please save them up for him and we will put his knowledge to the test! – No pressure there then Mark!

5. So, please give a warm welcome to Mark Rhodes.

This means the audience know there is a lot of good information coming their way, why they should listen to me, the fact that questions will be at the end and yes, it is OK to applaud as Mark comes to the front of the room.

It also means my credibility has been built with the audience already, so I don't have to do it myself. I always think someone starting by reading out their CV or their work history through the years is boring for the audience.

I do, of course, drop in relevant elements of my credibility throughout my talk to support the material or ideas I am sharing, but it serves two purposes. First off, it supports the concept I am talking about and reminds them of 'why me' to be presenting on this subject. For example, keeping with this 'Sales Talk' example, let's say I am talking about an element of sales that I call 'Confident and Definite' – a simple but very powerful concept that audiences might undervalue. I will add this 'dual purpose' credibility line to my talk:

'. . . and if you think this sounds too simple, well it is because of this very concept that I got airline x as a client, because two of their managers heard me talk about this, used it the next day with airline y and got this amazing outcome.'

The above also supports the second purpose, because it proves the simple technique I am explaining in my presentation does work and demonstrates the great results I help people to get.

Getting a great bio together is very important and you can't usually just roll out the same one; you need to tailor it to the specific audience, topic and event where your presentation will take place.

Practice and Preparation Starts as Soon as You Agree to a Talk

You've got to prepare enough so that you know your content well and how you are going to deliver it. You've got to practise so that all you need on the day are your bullet points (prompt notes) that tell you the content order and the appropriate story or worked example to use.

I practise my presentations a lot, especially when it's a new presentation.

But I have some presentations that are very similar and then I don't need to practise fully. I can just run through them very quickly on the morning of the talk because I've done them so many times.

I always practise my in-motion start and opening a lot, though, before any presentation and on the day in my head, because it is key to kicking things off on the right foot.

It never ceases to amaze me when people tell me they've delivered a bad presentation, or a presentation hasn't gone well.

I then ask how much preparation they did for the presentation and how long before the day did they know they had to do it. On average, people tell me they had between one and three months advance notice that the presentation was going to be needed. On average, people also tell me that preparation wise they had a busy week, so they just 'threw some slides together the night before'.

Well look, here's the problem. You should be thinking about that presentation as soon as you're asked to do it. You should start making notes, whether it's on your phone or in your notepad or elsewhere. Throughout the day, at various points, you carve out a bit of time. You think a bit more as you go through your own life experiences. During those two or three months things happen and you think, 'Oh, that will be a good story for my talk'. Or 'Oh, I need to talk about that in my talk'. And you build it over time.

When you get to the point where that talk is a couple of weeks away, you've got to be practising it. You've got to be going through that talk. Either the whole talk or just parts of it that you are not familiar with.

The thing is, in life people always want the results, but they don't want to put the work in or make the effort required. I've come off the stage at big events like Business Shows in London and I've had people come up to me and say: 'Mark, that was brilliant, that was fantastic. I wish I could do a talk like you'. Then, when I start talking to them, I find out their main problem is they don't practise. They just don't practise. They pull it all together at the last minute and then fumble through the presentation! It's no wonder they don't feel good about doing presentations. The preparation is very important.

Trust me, after a number of talks you'll have a catalogue of the 'tracks/segments' I spoke about earlier, and then you can massively reduce your practice and preparation time, but always be mindful of how much you should really do.

Delivering presentations is important, it positions you as an expert. It positions you as an influencer, and it's worth preparing for.

How do artists know how to sing songs? They sing them a lot.

How do sports stars get so good at their sport? They've practised a lot.

Yes, it can be boring to practise, but there's things we can do to reduce the boredom. Like only practising the bits we really need to, and then having a complete run through nearer the date.

Another thing I'll do is, let's say I have got to do a 45-minute talk, I'll do the whole thing through once with my fully detailed notes in front of me as a prompt, but I'll record it. And then – as sad as this might sound – I'll drive around in my car for a couple of weeks, and every now and then I'll play it and listen to it. As I listen to that recording a number of times, I'm learning the words to that presentation. And then my proper practice sessions are much easier. Remember, I am not learning a whole presentation but a series of 'bullet points/tracks or segments' – where, unlike song lyrics, they don't have to be repeated word for word on the day either.

This is how it's done. Not by waving a magic wand. You practise, and practise and practise. Then you know your content so well that you don't have to do as much practice in the future. But only when you've got it down and learnt it.

In the early days, you've got to practise it through and make the time to do it. I can't go on enough about practising. It's so, so important.

Of course, practice isn't the only issue; the content is often not interesting enough, which is why we covered that topic earlier in the book. When you get the content interesting, you've got that great 'in-motion' opening to walk up with and remove the hesitation gap, plus you've dealt with any perceived audience objections – all of which I covered earlier – then it is all so much easier.

Even if you are speaking to six people in a meeting room, you can have an 'in-motion' start as you go from your seat to the front of the room and then you're engaging the audience from the very beginning.

When you've got all those stories and you are starting with the outcome in mind that you want from the presentation, then you're telling them how they get there; you're also seeding it with interesting content and ideas, getting them to ask questions in their mind that get them thinking how you want them to think – then you've got everything working together in that presentation for you.

Timing

When you start to practise, you need to work through each track or bullet point from your prompt notes and note the timing. Timing is important, you cannot risk running out of time or overrunning your slot.

After I have got a good idea of what I am going to say for each track or bullet point, I then start to practise and record it on a phone app or voice recorder.

Initially I don't do the whole talk, I do it one track at a time. If my talk has 11 different tracks then I end up with 11 recordings, each one telling me how long it took, and I write the time in minutes next to each track on my prompt notes.

I then add them up and see if I have scope to expand my content further, because I am under time, or if I am over time I know I need to reduce some content somewhere.

The great thing about the multiple recordings technique is you can select a track and listen to it in isolation from the rest of the talk to decide how you could expand or reduce that section to achieve your overall timing goal. Let's say I am six minutes over. On reflection and reviewing my prompt notes and the recordings, there are four tracks I need to deal with as follows:

Track 3 – Currently five minutes
Track 5 – Currently two minutes
Track 6 – Currently six minutes
Track 9 – Currently four minutes – but now I want to say more and need six minutes.

I am certain all my other tracks are pretty fixed; no real opportunity to save time and no need to add anything else to them.

This means across tracks 3, 5, and 6 I need to lose a total of eight minutes (the six minutes I was already over and the extra two minutes I now know I need for Track 9).

I realise that Track 5 isn't really adding to the content so I delete it, now I need to save six minutes out of 11 minutes (Tracks 3 and 6). That's about 50%, so I listen to them again, go back to the original notes on the outcome of the talk and get very strict with making sure only content that contributes to the outcome is included.

I notice a few points in each presentation are there because I think they are funny but don't really add to the outcomes, so they go, and luckily this means I can lose three minutes from each of Tracks 3 and 6 giving me my timing. I then re-record these two tracks and I now have a complete set of recorded tracks that match the timing.

My aim now is to learn this, not necessarily word for word, but to a level where I know that just by using my track list of bullet points/prompt notes I will be able to deliver the rest of the content in the recording.

I edit my prompt sheet for the changes of track deletion and new timings and print a new copy.

On the day, I won't check my time against each item as I go. I will merely have two or three check points where on the prompt notes I will have what my accumulated time allowed is up to that point, and I can glance at my stopwatch to see how far ahead or behind I am and adjust my pace or level of detail accordingly for the rest of the presentation.

Now it's pretty common that some of the tracks you will find easy, you know the content well and don't need to practise them a lot. In that case, you just listen to the recordings of the ones you need to get better at and practise them until you are confident you can do that track, cover all the main points and do it in the time you have allowed.

Once you are comfortable with the more difficult tracks, you can then do a few full run throughs of the whole presentation and check your timings and keep doing that until you are confident with it.

I'm Still a Bit Nervous about Getting Started and Getting into My Flow

Sometimes people tell me they have their content nailed, they have done lots of practise, but despite having an 'in-motion' start to overcome the hesitation gap we covered earlier in the book, they feel they are going to struggle to get started and need time to get composed, organise their notes and other things once they get up to the front of the room.

What I advise in this case sounds a bit harsh, but it's what I call 'Put the audience under pressure'.

This technique is used to put pressure on the audience and take it off you to demonstrate you have control of the room.

Basically, you replace the 'in-motion' start with giving the audience something to do that you will be looking for their feedback and answers on.

You have been introduced from your bio, the warm welcome has been asked for, you walk up and just as the applause dies down (if there isn't any you can start as you are walking up) you say something like this:

> 'Right, before we get started I need you all to do something for me. I want you to get into twos or threes with the people next to you and between you make a list of the reasons why you think . . . then we will go round the room and see what some of you came up with.'

This buys you time to settle and your presentation has in many ways already started. After you have collected some feedback, you move into your main talk.

Now, a couple of things if you do this:

1. It needs to be relevant to the topic you are going to present on.
2. You need to adjust your timings of the rest of your material as this will take at least 10 minutes – five for them to work on it and five to get some answers back from the room.

I Don't Have Enough Content to Fill the Time Slot

If you are in the situation where you genuinely don't have enough content to fill your speaking slot, then the above interactive start is a good way to fill unused time allowance. If, like in my earlier example, you have dropped a few good stories to get to time, you might in the moment pull these back in to use up the extra time.

You can also, if needed, have another interactive and feedback segment just before your final wrap up, recap and ending.

The great thing is that no one needs to know, and you can do the end interactive if you have time left – as sometimes you will take more time than when you originally rehearsed it.

One thing I would say is do not have any interactives in the middle of your talk if you can help it. The reason is that these can really eat up time, especially when you get a real talkative person feeding back findings. Doing it at the start and end is best.

Slides

If you are using slides (I prefer not to) to support your presentation – remember they are there to support the presentation not you.

Keep the content on the slides to a minimum – maybe just a visual representation or key words.

I covered other considerations for using slides earlier in the book, but when it comes to preparation before the event, here are some key considerations:

1. Do you have to supply a laptop and/or projector?
2. If using your own laptop, what leads or connections are needed for the projector – is there an opportunity to test this before the day? Some equipment doesn't play well with Mac and/or Windows, so check this out too, including versions of Windows and ports like HDMI or VGA, etc.

3. If you are not using your own laptop, then what presentation software and versions do they use at the venue? Is it Mac or Windows? Is it PowerPoint or Keynote or something else? Are the slides to be formatted to 16:9 widescreen or square 4:3 or something else? There is nothing worse than arriving to find you need to reformat all your slides.

4. How will the slides be changed, will you use a remote, is one supplied?

5. Will you be able to see the slides on the laptop from where you present or will you have to keep turning to look at the big screen?

It is most important to take a print or handout of the slides with you on the day and be prepared and able to present without any slides. There is always a chance something will go wrong with slides, laptops and projectors, so you must be able to present without them, if you have to.

You need to arrive at the venue very early and test your slides out fully. There is nothing worse than an audience sitting waiting while a presenter is fumbling around looking for files and having issues getting the screen working. This loses all hope of removing the hesitation gap opening covered earlier in the book and eats up your time.

Microphones

Given your normal speaking or presenting volume, the audience size and room you'll be in, will you need to use a microphone?

If you do, then you need to know what types will be available.

→ *Is it a hand-held mic?* I avoid these at all costs as it restricts how animated I can be with my hands and I have to constantly focus on keeping it the same distance from my mouth for equal volume levels.

→ *Is it a lectern mic?* I would also avoid these at all costs as you have to stand behind the lectern and cannot move about too much.

→ *Is it a head mic?* This is my second choice, not too bad, you can wander about, they can sometimes be a little uncomfortable.

→ *Is it a lapel/clip on mic?* My favourite – you just have to remember not to rotate your head too far away from the mic when talking.

You must be at the venue on the day as early as possible, and certainly before audience members start arriving; you want to do a mic test and be familiar with it and what volume settings are going to work best. You also want to figure out if there are any points you can't walk to with the mic on that would cause feedback through the speakers. Not a pleasant experience for you or your audience when it happens.

Flip Charts

If you are using a flip chart, consider the audience size. On average, I say that above about 50 people a flip chart won't work, as not everyone will be able to see it.

The shape and size of the room dictates if it will work well or not so, like slides, you need to be prepared to do your presentation without a flip chart.

I never know until I arrive at a venue whether one will work. I have to write test words on the flip chart then walk round the outside of the room making sure every seat can see the words. This tells me how I need to move and position the flip chart, what colours will or won't work and how big my writing must be for people at the back corners to read it. If anyone can't read it, they will be distracted and distract the people around them by body movements to try and see and possibly by asking others around them 'Can you read that?'

Anything – including slides, flip charts, etc. – that is likely to be a problem for the audience should be avoided.

And if the venue is supplying the flip chart, then take your own paper and pens. I have rarely found a venue that has decent pens . . .

12
Delivering on the Day

Some 'delivering on the day items' were covered in the previous chapter, where we looked at slides, flip charts and mic tests. A number of the ideas in this chapter will seem really obvious when you read them, but you'll be surprised how many people do not do these simple things that can end up impacting their performance on the day due to last-minute panics or problems.

The Day Before You Travel to the Venue

The day before you travel you need everything ready:

Travel items, tickets, etc.
Clothes to wear on the day (see below)
Other clothes packed for the trip
Prompt notes printed
Slides printed and on a USB – even if emailed in advance
Paper, pens, anything else you need

Flip chart pens and paper, if you are using one
Print of the agenda and directions
Print of your bio for the person introducing you (this is a backup as you should have sent it to them way in advance of course).

You cannot leave any of this until the day you travel. What if your printer doesn't work? What if one of your items of clothing has a stain?

Travel

You should already have decided by now, based on the distance you have to travel and the time of your presentation, whether you need to travel the day before – or in some cases a number of days before.

You need to be able to guarantee you will arrive at the venue at least two hours before the event starts. You can check and test the equipment for mics and slides and get a feel for the venue and start to visualise in the actual room how you'll be delivering later in the day.

Prompt Notes

I always take two copies of my prompt notes that I print out the night before, so I have everything ready for the next day. These prompt notes are printed using a large enough font that I can easily read when glancing from a short distance, so I do not have to pick them up to read while presenting.

One copy is my backup copy, the other copy I mark up with any other points I don't want to forget – but these are in big and clear handwriting, easy to see and not a lot of small scribble.

For my prompt notes, I usually have three or four sheets of A4/US legal paper (one side printed) for a 1 hour talk. At the bottom of each page, I write the total of the times for that page and what the accumulated time should be on my stopwatch – so on page 1 these will be the same number. For example, if I have a 60-minute talk, I add up my timings on each page – worked out well before the event in my practice when recording and timing phases – and write at the bottom of the pages:

Page 1 – 20 minutes
Page 2 – 13 minutes
Page 3 – 22 minutes
Page 4 – 5 minutes

I don't actually write the word minutes, I write it like this:

Page 1 – 20→20
Page 2 – 13→33
Page 3 – 22→55
Page 4 – 5→60

The second number is the accumulated time.

Hence, I glance and check where I am at the end of each page, so if at the end of page 1 my stop watch says 18 minutes, I know I am ahead a little, and if it says 23 minutes I know I need to speed up or not spend so long on some areas.

So, what is the second set of prompt notes for? In case my first set goes missing – it has happened – in a break, or someone has moved them. Maybe I spill a drink on them, or I just make them messy by accident with notes and decide to work with my spare set instead and mark it up with timings, etc.

Timing

Getting the timing nailed is important; you cannot overrun and you certainly don't want to be one of those presenters using slides who says 'Sorry, running out of time so I am going to skip past some of these' then whizz past 20 slides to the final slide. That is bad, and the audience just think they have missed something.

If you are using slides, you need to be better at timing than when not using them. If you don't use slides you can easily adapt and even skip non-essential points because they are not on the screen for the audience to see! You just have to make sure you have sufficiently addressed everything in the talk overview, if one was issued, and have delivered what you promised in your opening comments.

You also need to check with the organiser or host on what happens if your presentation starts late – and you need to check these rules when you arrive, not just before you speak. Let's say you are due on 2–3 pm. Other presentations have run over and you can't start until 2:15 pm – do you still have your one-hour slot or are they likely to squeeze you down? You need to know this, especially if they have the dreaded timer person . . .

The Timer Person: Your Potential Problem

This you have to watch out for. You need to basically teach most of these people how timing will work for your presentation. You don't want to be doing your presentation, checking your stopwatch and confident to see you have 15 minutes left, and then see someone is holding up the 5-minute card!

This can happen for a number of reasons and it is difficult to deal with while doing your presentation, so you need the timer person to be on the ball. First, if you are starting late due to the event running late and you have been told you still have your full hour, make sure you tell the timer person that just before you speak. They may be looking at the agenda, see 3 pm is approaching, and flag you at 2:55 pm even though you didn't start until 2:15 pm – it happens, believe me.

The other thing that happens a lot, even if the event is running to time, is your stopwatch and the timer person's stopwatch saying different accumulated times, sometimes by as much 5 or 10 minutes!

How can that happen?

Well, usually because you start timing at different points. I tell them that I have an hour, so I will be starting my stopwatch as I start speaking – I actually do it as I am walking up after being introduced.

You see, what can happen is when someone else is introducing you and they welcome people back from lunch, then tell them what else is happening in the afternoon, perhaps then the plan for the evening, then eventually they read your bio (that you have given them way in advance, and taken a spare copy on the day of course!). Now, they could have taken 10 minutes or more to do all that, and you are now finally walking up and starting your stopwatch to time your hour. However, very often, unless you've had the talk with the timer person beforehand, they start timing your slot when the person that introduces you starts their piece – that has now taken 10 minutes!

You need to explain how you will time as soon as you get to the venue, and if they tell you the introduction is part of your slot then you need a commitment for the maximum length that intro will be and then reduce your own timings accordingly. (Luckily, we have that spare set of prompt notes!)

Other Things to Do When You Arrive at the Venue

→ *Mic and slide tests.* As mentioned earlier in the book, another advantage of arriving before the event starts is that if you need to use a mic and/or slides, you have the opportunity to test them out.
→ *Flip chart.* If you are using one of these, is it there, is there enough paper, are the pens any good? Good job you bought your own set and your own paper just in case!

Test that every seat in the room will be able to see the flip chart, move it around, write on it in different sizes and different colours. Then walk the entire four corners of the room and make sure you can read all of it, or at least know how big you need to write and what colours do and don't work given the distance and lighting, etc.

However, the most important thing I do when I arrive at the venue is get used to the room and the speaking area or stage. I need to check a few things – first, is there a table for my notes, stopwatch and water? If not, I need to get that arranged.

The other thing I do is practise how I will walk up, place my notes, water and stopwatch, and then how and where I will walk when talking. I look for any barriers or pillars in the room that may cause audience members to struggle to see me if I stand in certain positions.

I rehearse the first few minutes of my presentation a number of times, from my introduction ending. So I start walking up, imagine applause fading and then begin my 'in-motion' start, place my notes, stopwatch and water while I am still doing it, and then move to a position away from the notes and go into my presentation.

For me, I don't practise this out loud – I am usually doing it in my head or whispering it to myself, getting a feel of the room, how I will walk and talk and animate different aspects of my presentation, while making eye contact with the audience, making sure I go to each end of the stage if it is very wide, so all audience members feel included.

I make sure when doing this walking practice that I am looking out for where the chairs are, scanning the audience positions to remind me that later – when I am presenting – I need to keep looking at the audience to keep them engaged.

In this practice session I also walk back to the table at times and practise glancing at my notes, making sure I can easily see them. If I have problems, I may need to move the table for better lighting or ask for better lighting in the room.

All of this advance planning is necessary to make sure you minimise anything that could disrupt you or your presentation once it starts.

I do all of this early, before the event starts; usually there will be very few, if any, people there. If there are any breaks or lunch before my slot, I will do this again in the break nearest my slot.

The Presentations Before Yours

Even if you are speaking at the end of the day and it is an all-day event, you want to be there before it starts. Get a feel for the room and the audience through the day and how they react to the presentations before yours. This also gives you an opportunity to make other notes or amend your notes based on what happens in any presentations before yours. Obviously, if you are doing anything with slides, you don't want to have to change your slides last minute.

I will often refer back to things other presenters have said. I never disagree with anything another presenter has said – even if I don't agree with it. I only add positive references where we align.

If another presenter has said something that conflicts with something I was going to say, then I either:

1. Take it out of my presentation – remembering that may impact slides, although I rarely use them.

2. Address it in my presentation by simply saying 'Different things work for different people and one of the things I have found/experienced/seen, etc. is . . . ' (I never refer to the other presentation though).

Voice Control

Voice control becomes a problem if you're not speaking loud enough or you get nervous. A lot of voice issues are caused by a dry mouth while speaking. Nerves can cause a dry mouth, so have lots of water available. I drink about half a bottle of water while I'm being introduced and I drink a lot of water just before I go up.

I also make sure that in the hour before I'm presenting I don't drink any tea or coffee, because I've found they make my mouth dry out about five minutes into a presentation. Whereas, if I drink half a bottle of water – I'm talking about half of one of those small bottles of water – before I talk then I normally don't need to take any water during a 60-minute presentation and my mouth doesn't dry out.

If you do get a dry mouth, just have some water there and take it as needed.

13
Final Thoughts: What Will Being Better at Presentations Mean to You?

If you want to get better at doing presentations; if you want to reduce that fear; if you want to deliver great presentations that people not only love and enjoy but also have them take the action that you want them to take from it – then you need to think what the impact on your life is going to be of being able to do all that. How much will it transform things for you?

And the answer is probably 'massively'.

So it's going to be worth the effort of making the changes. It's going to be worth the effort of practising.

If you've got to practise, and you want to practise in front of people, join something like Toastmasters. Toastmasters is a not-for-profit group that's set up branches all around the world where like-minded people who want to get great at delivering presentations meet up. They deliver presentations in front of each other and give each other constructive help. But the biggest thing I think they do is give you a room of people to practise your material on and practise presenting to. I didn't go the Toastmasters route myself, and for some people it doesn't work and for others it's brilliant. Just something to explore.

You know, in my own life, I've cracked it now – I do it well (so I am told) and love every minute of it. However, thinking about all the opportunities I missed out on by not doing presentations in earlier years haunts me to this day. For instance, when I had my software company, we would sell our software projects for between £50 000 and £250 000. I would often attend conferences where we'd have 300 potential customers in the room, and my Finance Director would say to me: 'Mark, we've got a great opportunity. You can go on stage for a couple of minutes and tell 300 people about what we do and how great we are, and maybe we'll get some more business from the audience'.

I wouldn't do it.

What I regret, looking back, is how many new client opportunities did I miss? What if, out of those 300 people in the audience, there was one, just one, that if they heard me speak would eventually buy our system? That could be £100 000 or maybe £200 000!

And how many talks have I avoided doing? It was probably 50 talks over the years! I'm not even going to work out the sum of 50 times £100 000. I'm not even going to work it out, as it would scare me to death.

Being able to present and do presentations that you love doing and the audience love hearing is one of the most rewarding and satisfying things you can do in your life – even if you are not doing it to make money at the end of the day. Just being able to do it and enjoy it and at the same time help others is immensely rewarding.

It can also make you stand out from colleagues!

If you're not yet at that stage, then applying the ideas and strategies in this book will help you get there. Get the help and get it done because you will never look back. And you'll be proud of yourself every time you deliver a presentation.

That's the biggest thing I get these days out of doing presentations. Being able to look back and think, 'Wow, in the past I'd never have done that. I'd never spoken in front of 1000 people. How far I have come'.

When I'm coming off stage, and I've got a standing ovation, I'm thinking, 'Wow, did I just do that?'

It's amazing. You might not want to take presenting and public speaking to that level, but whatever it is that you want to do with public speaking, the techniques in this book are going to take you there.

Even if you are part of a team, you're an employee and you're working for someone else – if you're the person in your team or in your company that can stand up and do a presentation, you become highly valuable to that company, because most people won't do it.

And normally, most of those who will do it, don't do it very well.

If you develop this skill, you'll make yourself very difficult to replace – no matter what it is you do – if speaking and presentations are part of the business or the opportunity that you're involved in.

I wish you huge success in developing your ability to deliver presentations and talks your audience will love and you will enjoy doing.

Mark

Mark Rhodes

Website: https://www.markrhodes.com

Twitter: @rhodes2success

YouTube: https://www.youtube.com/massivelyimprove

Videos to support this book: https://www.markrhodes .com/public-speaking-videos

Index